Twayne's United States Authors Series

EDITOR OF THIS VOLUME

Kenneth Eble

University of Utah

Albert Maltz

TUSAS 311

Albert Maltz

ALBERT MALTZ

By JACK SALZMAN
Hofstra University

TWAYNE PUBLISHERS
A DIVISION OF G. K. HALL & CO., BOSTON

Library of Congress Cataloging in Publication Data

Salzman, Jack.
  Albert Maltz.

  (Twayne's United States authors series ; 311)
  Bibliography: p. 153–57
  Includes index.
  1. Maltz, Albert, 1908–   —Criticism and interpretation.
PS3525.A49Z8   818'.5'209   78–2403
ISBN 0–8057–7228–6

Contents

About the Author

Preface

Acknowledgments

Chronology

1. "Merry Go Round"   15
2. A Workers' Theater   22
3. The Way Things Were   33
4. *We Hold These Truths*   45
5. A Moment in an American Winter   54
6. The Hollywood Years   72
7. "The Path of Man"   104
8. A Long Journey   118
9. Maltz Reestablished   138
   Notes and References   141
   Selected Bibliography   153
   Index   158

About the Author

Jack Salzman is Professor of English and Director of the American Studies Program at Hofstra University. He has been a Fulbright lecturer in Finland and Japan. Professor Salzman is also editor of *Prospects: An Annual of American Cultural Studies.* His publications include: *Years of Protest, The Survival Years* and *Theodore Dreiser: The Critical Reception.*

Preface

In a short sketch of himself which he wrote in 1942 for *Twentieth-Century Authors,* Albert Maltz noted:

My father came to this country as a boy from what is now Lithuania, and followed the usual course of immigrants — that of laborious work from childhood in a desperate attempt to gain security — and then to keep it. He was a grocer's boy, a salesman, later a house painter, and for some years, a farmer. In middle life he became a successful builder. He went to a comparatively early grave, worn out, carrying with him a love for America and painter's lead poisoning. My mother came to this country as an infant from Poland. She wanted to be a school teacher and spent her adolescent years instead as a seamstress in a sweatshop. There she contracted trachome, and the girl who wanted to be a schoolteacher lived out the rest of her life unable to read. That too I have remembered.[1]

Years later, the tone of outrage would no longer seem valid, and Maltz would comment in a letter that "there are enough things wrong with the American social system without attempting to indict it for the wrong reasons."[2] Despite his change of attitude, Maltz's sketch is of considerable interest because it is clearly marked by the voice of a writer who was very much a product of the Great Depression and who was to become one of the mainstays of the literary Left in the 1930s.

American literature, of course, always has been a literature of protest. And so it was in the 1930s — only more so. Indeed, if there is any one characteristic that particularizes the literature of the thirties it is the extreme form of the protest. Yet, paradoxically, the protest is not only more extreme than American literary protest had been prior to the 1930s; it is also more hopeful. The stock market crash of October, 1929, gave a specific point of focus to what previously had been a general feeling of discontent; the failure of the American Dream was now to be seen most dramatically in the exploitation of the proletariat. And as a result, as William Phillips and Philip Rahv have noted, "the atmosphere of American literature became more political than at any other time in its history."[3] A sense of social outrage finally became combined with a feeling of political expectation. To overcome the platitudes and apparent indifference of Herbert Hoover — to overcome the lie that "no one has starved" — demanded nothing less than a revolution. A new world had to be built, and in the early 1930s only the Communist Party seemed capable of providing a central force around which these dreamers of a new world could organize.

For the writers on the Left, the building of a new world necessitated the reevaluation of the role of the artist. At issue was the question of how the artist was to help in the creation of the new order, whether he was to consider his art as a weapon to be used in the establishment of "a new world from which the evils endangering mankind will have been uprooted, and in which the foundations will live for the creating of a universal human culture."[4]

In 1930, two seminal statements were issued that dramatically foreshadowed the importance that this concept of the artist would assume throughout most of the decade. Sinclair Lewis, in accepting the Nobel Prize on December 12, 1930, denounced the purveyors of the genteel tradition, and expressed his sorrow that he was a little too old to join the young American writers "who are doing such passionate and authentic work" and who were finally bringing American literature out of the "stuffiness of safe, sane, and incredibly dull provincialism."[5] One of the writers whom Lewis singled out for special praise was Michael Gold, editor of *New Masses,* author of *Jews Without Money,* and acknowledged to be America's leading advocate of proletarian literature. Just two months prior to Lewis's acceptance speech, *The New Republic* had published Gold's review of four novels and a volume of plays by Thornton Wilder in which Gold had castigated Wilder as the poet of the "genteel bourgeoisie."[6] To Gold, a writer's obligation was to the Cause not to his craft, and he attacked Wilder for creating not a world but a museum, "an historical junkshop . . . [whose] goal is comfort and status quo." Gold's comments precipitated a heated controversy, the significance of which was first noted by Edmund Wilson almost two years later: "There is no question," Wilson wrote in May, 1932, "that the Gold-Wilder row marked definitely the eruption of the Marxist issues out of the literary circles of the radicals into the field of general criticism. After that, it became very plain that the economic crisis was to be accompanied by a literary one.''[7]

The literary class war was to dominate the American literary scene for most of the Depression decade, and Albert Maltz was one of the pivotal figures in the controversy; few voices on the Left were as articulate and rational as his. Less than ten years later, Maltz became involved in another bitter battle when, as one of The Hollywood Ten, he joined the struggle for freedom of expression against the insidious power of the House Committee on Un-American Activities. Yet today, Maltz, like many writers of the literary Left, is virtually a forgotten figure. The only full-length study devoted to his work was written by an East German scholar, Eberhard Brüning, and has never appeared in this country. Moreover, as the bibliography at the end of this volume makes clear, little attention has been given to Maltz's work either in literary histories or scholarly articles. (In the *Literary History of the United States,* for example, Maltz's name is mentioned only once.) And with the exception of *Afternoon in the Jungle,* a volume of short stories which was published in 1971, none of Maltz's work is in print and few of his books are to be found in libraries.

The aim of this study, therefore, is to introduce the reader to the works and times of Albert Maltz. Because his writings are not generally available, more space has been allotted to a summary of the plays, stories, and novels than would have been necessary had the works been accessible. And because Maltz was a central figure in several controversies, considerable attention is given to them, as well as to the conditions that precipitated the controversies. By so doing I hope to make clear that Maltz was a far more significant figure in the history of American letters than is generally acknowledged. (Indeed, the continued neglect of Maltz and other writers of the Left at the same time that we continue to hunt for the minutiae of Washington Irving and reprint the works of William Gilmore Simms, is one of the glaring failures of American literary scholarship.)

JACK SALZMAN

Hofstra University

Acknowledgments

My thanks are due to Karen Corti, who helped type the manuscript in its early stages; Joseph Duchac, who typed the final version; Kenneth A. Lohf, Librarian for Rare Books and Manuscripts, Columbia University, and Josephine L. Harper, Manuscripts Curator of The State Historical Society of Wisconsin, who kindly provided me with copies of Maltz's works in their collections; The Brooklyn Center Committee on Research of Long Island University, which provided me with financial aid and released time from teaching duties; Ben Bengal, Paul Peters, George Sklar, John Wexley, and Victor Wolfson, with whom I spent several pleasant afternoons; and, most of all, to Albert Maltz, who gave most generously of his time, knowledge, and interest.

Chronology

1908   Albert Maltz born October 28 in Brooklyn, New York.

1926   Graduated Erasmus Hall High School in Brooklyn.

1926– Attended Columbia College; received B.A. and elected to
1930   Phi Beta Kappa.

1931   Attended Yale University's School of Drama, where he studied with George Pierce Baker and Alexander Dean. Met George Sklar, a fellow student, and began collaborating on "Merry Go Round."

1932   "Merry Go Round" opened April 22 at Provincetown Theatre; after two weeks the production moved uptown and played for an additional six weeks.

1933   *Peace on Earth* written with Sklar; became a member of the Executive Board of the newly formed Theatre Union, which accepted *Peace on Earth* as its first production; the play opened on November 29 and ran for eighteen weeks.

1934   On March 18 Maltz and Sklar awarded the Annie E. Gray Peace Plaque for the "outstanding American work of art contributing most to the cause of peace." Maltz began trip through Pennsylvania and West Virginia in search of material on Mother Jones, an early twentieth-century organizer of coal miners.

1935   *Black Pit* opened March 20 at Civic Repertory Theatre; "Private Hicks" awarded first prize in New Theatre League's contest for a one-act play against war and fascism. "Man on a Road" published in *New Masses* on January 8.

1936   "Game" published in December issue of *Scribner's;* "Good-by" published in *New Masses* on December 15.

1937   Married Margaret Larkin. Became a part-time instructor of playwriting at New York University where he taught until 1941. Published "Letter from the Country" (*New Masses,* August 17); "Hotel Raleigh, the Bowery" (*Story,* September); "Incident on a Street Corner" (*New Yorker,* November 27). "Hotel Raleigh, the Bowery" dramatized by Philip

Stevenson; under the title, "Transit," was produced the following year.

1938 "Rehearsal" opened at Detroit Contemporary Theatre on May 26; "The Happiest Man on Earth," published in *Harper's* in June, awarded first prize in the O. Henry Memorial Awards; "Hotel Raleigh, the Bowery," now called "Season of Celebration," included in *The Flying Yorkshireman,* a Book-of-the-Month Club selection; *The Way Things Are* published by International.

1939 Helped organize and became one of the editors of *Equality;* contributed statement on anti-Semitism to *We Hold These Truths,* and wrote an unsigned prefatory essay to the booklet; taught at the Writers' Conference in the Rocky Mountains at the University of Colorado (1939–40).

1940 *The Underground Stream* published by Little, Brown; "Sunday Morning on Twentieth Street" published in *Southern Review.* With George Sklar rewrote *Peace on Earth* for a theater group in Los Angeles, which presented the play as "Zero Hour."

1941 Moved to Los Angeles; "Afternoon in a Jungle" published in *New Yorker,* January 11.

1942 With W. R. Burnett wrote screenplay for *This Gun for Hire;* edited and wrote commentary for short film, *Moscow Strikes Back,* which received an award as the best foreign documentary from the Academy of Motion Picture Arts and Sciences.

1943 Collaborated with Delmar Daves on film, *Destination Tokyo.*

1944 *The Cross and the Arrow* published by Little, Brown.

1945 Wrote script for *Pride of the Marines;* received Academy Award for *The House I Live In,* a film short.

1946 Collaborated with Ring Lardner, Jr., on *Cloak and Dagger;* "What Shall We Ask of Writers?" printed in *New Masses* on February 12.

1947 Became president of the Western Regional Council of the Authors League of America. On October 28 testified before The House Committee on Un-American Activities.

1948 Collaborated with Marvin Wald on *The Naked City.*

1949 *The Journey of Simon McKeever* published by Little, Brown.

1950 On April 23 delivered address, "On the Eve of Prison," at a rally in Los Angeles; in June was committed to the federal jail in Washington, D.C.; the following month was moved to the federal prison camp in Mill Point, West Virginia. "Circus Come to Town" published in July issue of *Masses & Mainstream*. *The Citizen Writer: Essays in Defense of American Culture* published by International. Received Silver Award of the Commonwealth Club of California for *The Journey of Simon McKeever.*

1951 Released from jail in April; "The Whiskey Men" published in November issue of *Masses & Mainstream.*

1952 Received the Normandy Pen Award; "The Morrison Case" produced in Leipzig and Berlin.

1953 *The Cross and the Arrow* ordered removed from libraries of the United States Information Service abroad; many libraries in the United States removed all his books from their shelves.

1956 *A Long Day in a Short Life* published by International.

1960 Hired and fired by Frank Sinatra to write the screenplay of *The Execution of Private Slovik.* "With Laughter" published in *Southwest Review* under the name of Julian Silva; *Off-Broadway,* a collection of stories, published in East Germany.

1961 "Husband and Wife," unpublished in the United States, adapted for television under the title "The Great Alberti"; "With Laughter" received award as best story published in *Southwest Review* for 1960–1961.

1964 Divorced from Margaret Larkin. Married Rosemary Wylde.

1966 *A Tale of One January* published in Great Britain by Calder & Boyers.

1968 Two stories published in *Saturday Evening Post:* "The Prisoner's Dog" (July) and "The Spoils of War" (October). Death of wife, Rosemary.

1969 Married Esther Engelberg.

1970 *Two Mules for Sister Sara* released.

1971 *Afternoon in the Jungle: Selected Stories of Albert Maltz* published by Liveright.

CHAPTER 1

"Merry Go Round"

T HE start of Albert Maltz's career as a dramatist coincided with the onset of the Great Depression. In 1930, Maltz, who had been born twenty-two years earlier in Brooklyn, New York, graduated from Columbia College and decided to enroll in Yale University's Drama School to study with the renowned George Pierce Baker (whose students at Harvard had included Eugene O'Neill, S. N. Behrman, Sidney Howard, and Thomas Wolfe).[1] Baker's impact on Maltz was considerable. But, even more formidable, was the influence of Alexander Dean and a fellow student, George Sklar.

From Dean, a Professor of Directing, Maltz learned about the workings of the theater; he was a man, Maltz has commented, "who knew more about theater in all phases" than anyone else he has met.[2] Sklar exerted a different kind of influence. When Maltz entered Yale he was, by his own account, a "pacifist humanist"; Sklar was somewhat more politically oriented, and their talks soon convinced Maltz that "individuals live not in a vacuum but in society, and that a writer cannot write truly of people or characters unless the world in which they live is equally illuminated."[3] The talks between the two students led to their becoming good friends. And in 1931, while still attending classes, Maltz and Sklar began to collaborate on a play, "Merry Go Round," which to their delight was produced the following year.

When "Merry Go Round" first opened, reviewers saw what they took to be a parallel between the events in the play and the slaying of the notorious gambler, Arnold Rothstein.[4] The similarities notwithstanding, however, "Merry Go Round" was inspired not by the murder of Rothstein but by a gangland slaying in Cleveland. In

15

the fall of 1931, George Sklar, who was working part-time in the Yale Library, came upon an article that told of a gangland slaying in Cleveland that had been accidentally witnessed by a laborer, who reported the shooting to the police. According to the account given in the article, the gangsters had been involved with the city administration and it was decided that the witness would have to be kept quiet. He was taken to jail as a material witness, where he was found hanged, an alleged suicide. Sklar showed the magazine article to Maltz, who agreed that it would make an exciting play. That day they completed the outline, and in the spring of 1932 they left Yale for the New York production of their first play.

I   *To Shame, To Preach*

"Merry Go Round," as Stark Young wrote in his review for *The New Republic,* means "to shame and exhort, to preach."⁵ But it is not a work of propaganda. Although Maltz and Sklar wanted to expose the corruption of the political machine, as well as the brutality of the police, they used the political situation primarily for its theatrical value. "Merry Go Round" is interesting melodrama, which falters, when it does, not from any intrusion of an ideological stance but from weak characterization and a lack of subtlety. (By 1952, Maltz came to regard the lack of an ideological position as perhaps the weakest aspect of the play. In a letter to Maximilian Scheer, an East German who was translating "Merry Go Round," Maltz noted that when the play had been written he and Sklar "were still moving toward those forces in society which ultimately will cleanse our country. Neither politically nor artistically nor spiritually were we as yet integrated with those elements.... It would seem to me of the utmost importance now for the story of this play to indicate that other factors exist in society — that while it is true that innocent pawns suffer and die in the United States, at the same time there are organized forces which struggle against this and will one day put an end to it."⁶)

II   *Walker's Merry Go Round*

For several months prior to the production of "Merry Go Round," an investigation — ordered by the state legislature and headed by Samuel Seabury — had been under way in New York regarding corruption in the city government in general and the link between gangsters and politicians in particular. Mayor James J. Walker, who eventually had fifteen charges leveled against him, was in an extremely precarious position, and in fact was only a few months away from suddenly resigning his office and leaving for Europe to avoid a summons for a personal investigation of his affairs by the then-Governor of New York, Franklin D. Roosevelt.[7] The apparent similarities between the New York political situation and the events in "Merry Go Round" eventually came to the attention of the Walker administration, and an attempt was made to prevent the play from being produced.[8]

The producers of "Merry Go Round" did not have enough money at first to open the play on Broadway, and with the consent of Maltz and Sklar they opened instead at the small Provincetown Playhouse. They had done the same thing the previous year with another play, I. J. Golden's *Precedent,*[9] which, after garnering several favorable critical reviews, had received offers to move to Broadway. The hope, of course, was that the same fate would befall "Merry Go Round." And, in fact, that is exactly what happened: the play got a good press, and the following day offers were received from nine Broadway theater owners to move the play uptown.

A deal was made with the Leblang Agency to move "Merry Go Round" to Broadway after the contract with Provincetown, which called for a two-week run, had expired. But within a few days the Leblang Agency decided that it did not want to go through with the deal, and a quick check disclosed that seven of the other theater owners also had changed their minds about leasing their theaters for the production of "Merry Go Round." The explanation was always the same: "Sorry, but we just booked another play into our theater."[10] The ninth owner, however, agreed to stand by his offer, and plans were made to open the play at the 45th Street Avon Theatre.

Opening night came, and so did the police. They blocked the entrance to the Avon and announced that the play could not be performed because the theater did not have a current license from the Fire Department. As some inquiries soon made clear, the previous year's license had indeed expired; but so too had the licenses of at least two other theaters on the same street. There was, in fact, a frequent gap between the expiration of the old license and the issuance of a new one. This technicality, however, was used to prevent only "Merry Go Round" from opening; no attempt was made to have the performances cancelled at the other theaters. When this became known, the producers of "Merry Go Round" decided to hire an attorney, the Civil Liberties Union became interested in the case, and for several days the story was front-page news in the city's newspapers.

When Mayor Walker was queried by reporters about the incident, he told them: "I know nothing about it, but I hear it's a lousy play anyway." Nonetheless, editorial criticism continued to be severe, and in an apparent attempt to save face the Fire Department insisted that all the curtains in the theater be fireproofed and a dozen rows of seats removed to provide an orchestra pit — even though the play did not call for an orchestra. The ordinances were complied with, and on May 10, one week after the originally scheduled opening, "Merry Go Round" was allowed to appear on Broadway.

III   *Ed Martin, Bellhop*

"Merry Go Round" begins with a darkened stage. Only the noise of a big city is heard, and the moving lights of a sign on a building announcing the latest news are all that is seen. The headlines read: "WHEAT FALLS TO NEW LOW.... HOOVER ORDERS CONFIDENCE AS SOLUTION FOR DEPRESSION.... WINCHESTER REPORT OF LAW ENFORCEMENT PUBLISHED TOMORROW.... KID CHOCOLATE WINS .... CITIZENS COMMITTEE DEMANDS INVESTIGATION OF CRIME — FEELING RUNS HIGH AT CONTINUED GANG VIOLENCE."[11] From the very beginning of the play, the effects of the Depression are thus set off against the corruption of the political system.

As the lights come up on stage, the scene is that of the bellhops' locker room in a large metropolitan hotel. Ed Martin — the counterpart of the Cleveland laborer who had witnessed the gangland slaying — is talking to two other hops. A phone call for service interrupts the conversation, and Ed hurries to respond. The call is from Jake Stransky, the most notorious of the gangsters staying at the hotel, and, anticipating a big tip, Ed starts for Stransky's room, pleased that it "looks like the breaks for one night anyway." But Stransky has been set up to be murdered, and young Martin is in the room when Jig Zelli breaks in and shoots Stransky. Ed tries to run out of the room, but he too is shot. As cries of "Open up there'' are heard, Zelli escapes out the window, angered that he has only wounded the bellhop.

When he regains consciousness, Ed refuses to name the assailant. Afraid to talk, he is taken into custody as a material witness. But he refuses to give the police the information they want: "What sense is there to it?'' he asks one of the detectives. "What the hell have I got to do with it? Why should I take the chance of gettin' bumped off for something I don't have a thing to do with?'' The grilling continues; the police get tougher and nastier. Finally, Ed is warned that *"Somebody's* gotta take the rap for this, and if you don't help us get the right man it may be you.'' The point is made: Ed picks Zelli's photograph from several which have been handed him. The police are elated, and the young bellhop is assured that they will protect him — that they will "play square'' with him.

Coincidentally, Stransky's murder takes place just when a bill to investigate corruption in the state's politics is up before the legislature. The Tammany leaders are convinced that the only chance they have to prevent passage of the bill is to pull something fast. An immediate conviction in the Stransky case, they decide, would show that the police and local politicians really are doing something for the people and would give the Governor some reason for vetoing the bill. So Ed is once again asked to identify Zelli as Jake Stransky's murderer, and the police call for the Grand Jury. But before the Grand Jury can be convened, Zelli shows the police photostats of some papers he had taken from Stransky after he shot him: "I'm going to be outa this can in a shot or I'll know why,'' Zelli warns the police. "And if you think I'm bluffin', just try and call me.... Unless you want the great wide world to know what mayor of what City owns a silent partnership in what speakcasy and why, and what public official borrowed ten grand from Stransky on the twelfth of November and why, and who hired a mob of gunmen to break up what clothing strike and why ... and a couple hundred other little items like that.... Well, yuh better do some agreein' and do it fast.'' Zelli's disclosure that he has Stransky's records has just the effect he expects, and the first act of "Merry Go Round'' ends with the Mayor, the Tammany leaders, and the hangers-on shouting "Quash the indictment.''

In Act II, a bewildered Ed Martin is told that his testimony is no longer needed. He is worried, though, because he has lost his job at the hotel and is afraid that the Depression will make it difficult for him to find another one. The Mayor promises him a letter of reference, and Ed decides that it would be a good time for him to move with his wife to New York. But the Tammany people are still troubled by the pending investigation, and they are more determined than ever to get an immediate conviction in the Stransky case: it's the "one chance of taking the wind out of that investigation." Ed Martin is chosen as the scapegoat: "He identified Zelli," the assistant District Attorney announces, "to save his own neck." Ed is arrested just as he is getting ready to leave for New York, and this time he is beaten until he agrees to sign a confession.

The sense of outrage that one feels at the betrayal of the bellhop is intensified in the last act by the indifference of the police: "Well, it's all in the game," says a sergeant standing over Ed's badly beaten body. And when one of the detectives remarks that there are times when he wishes he "wasn't in the racket" he is summarily told to "get yourself some guts, willya Beachley." The police are reluctant even to allow Ed to be taken to the hospital, insisting that "he isn't the first bird that's got a message here." But the doctor examining Ed warns that he's taken a bad beating — "He's not a mug who'll stand anything" — and the police finally take him to the hospital.

The beating attracts the attention of a lawyer, Harry Berger, who publicly charges that the bellhop was framed and that third degree methods were used to extract the confession. With an election at hand, the party bosses decide that something once again must be done to squelch the investigation. Ed Martin must be found dead in his cell; that way "he won't have to stand trial, and he'll stand convicted too, and Berger won't have anything to go on." A final headline announces their success: BELLBOY CONFESSES GUILT BY SUICIDE. The mayor wins the election by a majority of 100,000 votes, and in a cliché-filled speech declares:

> It is with no small sense of my responsibility that I have accepted the renomination for Mayor. I cannot have been Mayor of a great city like this for four years without fully realizing the burden that the office entails. To take upon myself the trust of millions of people is no small matter. To accept willingly the praise and blame for the honest administration of a city government is no light task. But I know all this, and, knowing it, I have nevertheless agreed to take it all upon myself again and to work, unstintingly, unselfishly, devotedly, to the best of my ability, in the best interests of this great public I hope to serve again.

As the speech is concluded nothing is seen but the silhouette of Ed Martin hanging in his cell.

IV   Afraid to Talk

Maltz and Sklar had been hopeful that the publicity attendant upon the Broadway opening of "Merry Go Round" would help the play have a long run. But, despite the good reviews and the fact that the play had attracted packed houses at the Provincetown, the Broadway production did poorly from the very beginning. There were inadequate funds to promote the play, the theater was not air-conditioned, and the publicity attached to the closing of the theater may have made people fearful that there would be trouble if they went to the Avon. Whatever the exact reasons may have been, audiences were very small and "Merry Go Round" closed after six weeks.[12] The following year Universal Pictures made it into an undistinguished film called *Afraid to Talk*.

CHAPTER 2

A Workers' Theater

AFTER the closing of "Merry Go Round," Maltz and Sklar went to Hollywood, where they were hired to do the treatment of a film script (not *Afraid to Talk*). The treatment was not found acceptable, their option was not renewed, and three months after their arrival in Hollywood, Maltz and Sklar were on their way back to New York. Upon their return, Sklar, who earlier had learned about a theater group that was being formed which would "present plays that deal boldly with the economic and social problems that confront all of us today,"[1] called Charles Walker, the treasurer of the newly formed Theatre Union, who invited both Sklar and Maltz to join the Executive Board of the new organization.[2] With the Theatre Union in mind Maltz and Sklar then began to work on their second play, *Peace on Earth*.

I The Theatre Union

In an article in the *Daily Worker* entitled, "The Need for a Workers' Theatre," the two playwrights explained why the Theatre Union had been organized: "The Broadway theatre of today," they wrote, "is a class theatre — a theatre existing solely for the amusement of the so-called upper classes — a parlor theatre dealing with parlor problems — an escape theatre — a sterile theatre." A new kind of theater was needed, one which would "reflect the fact that we're living in a certain type of society, a society gripped by the most severe economic crisis that capitalism has known." The very future of theater in America, the playwrights argued, rested in the creation of a workers' theater, a theater like the Theatre Union whose "purpose is to produce plays about the working class, writ-

ten from the point of view of the interests of the working class —
where workers can attend plays at prices they can afford and where
the theatre is not a form of titillation but is a moving cultural force,
dramatic and alive.''[3]

The Theatre Union was, in fact, a somewhat unique institution in
the American theater. To be sure, it was not the only group to produce plays of social protest: the Group Theatre, Artef, the Federal
Theatre, and the Theatre of Action brought a new and exciting
dimension to the concept of drama as a social force.[4] But the
Theatre Union was the first professional social theater in the
United States; and although it was a professional theater, it was set
up on a nonprofit basis with the specific purpose of producing
plays that were socially significant. Its orientation was socialist,
and its Executive Board was composed of both theater people and
men and women whose background was that of political organization in trade unions and left-wing mass organizations. It was the
first professional theater to attempt to attract working people to its
plays — and succeeded in doing so. Tickets were priced from thirty-
five cents to a maximum of $1.50, and free tickets were given to
members of organizations of the unemployed; theater parties were
developed to a degree previously unknown; and it was the first
theater in the history of New York to open its orchestra seating to
Blacks (who previously could purchase balcony seats only).[5]

After it took over Eva Le Gallienne's off-Broadway Civic Repertory Theatre in 1933, the Theatre Union produced seven plays
before it disbanded four years later. The first production was *Peace
on Earth,* which opened on November 29, 1933, and ran for eighteen weeks. Subsequent works included Paul Peters and George
Sklar's *Stevedore,* the most financially successful of the seven
plays; Friedrich Wolf's *Sailors of Cattaro;* a second play by Maltz,
Black Pit; Paul Peters' adaptation of Bertolt Brecht's *Mother;*[6]
Albert Bein's *Let Freedom Ring;* Victor Wolfson's *Bitter Stream;*
and John Howard Lawson's *Marching Song.* Lawson's play
opened on February 17, 1937, and was the last of the Theatre
Union's productions. Unlike the six previous productions, *Marching Song* was presented at the Nora Bayes Theatre rather than at
the Civic Repertory. (The bank that owned the Civic Repertory
Theatre demanded a rent increase that was higher than the Theatre
Union could pay; the building that housed the Civic Repertory was
subsequently torn down and turned into a parking lot.)

It was at this time, too, that Charles Walker, the organization's principal money raiser, decided to withdraw from the Executive Board. The group was already split because of political differences, and with a sparsity of good manuscripts with which to work and without Walker to help defray the large accumulation of debts, the Theatre Union found it impossible to continue. In June, 1937, Margaret Larkin was asked to write an article for the newspapers announcing the termination of the group, and after that it was largely a matter of trying to pay off the outstanding debts. Little fuss was made about the demise of the Theatre Union, although the following year Robert Forsythe wrote wistfully, "Whenever a new theatrical season starts I get a yearning for the old Theatre Union down on Fourteenth Street. The place had been well known when Eva Le Gallienne had her Civic Repertory Theatre there but it really got in swing when the Theatre Union began blowing the roof off with radical plays. For a time plays were put on in which ideas were expressed in the most violent fashion and without concern that somebody in ermine might be offended."[7]

II   Peace on Earth

Peace on Earth, the second and last work on which Albert Maltz and George Sklar collaborated, is a more political work than "Merry Go Round." It is an anti-war play — with the time of the events prophetically set "in a year or so" — and it may well be the first American play to attack war as the inevitable result of a capitalistic system.[8] As in "Merry Go Round," the system destroys those who oppose it; and like Ed Martin, Peter Owens, a college teacher and the central figure in *Peace on Earth,* is murdered by a corrupt society: his opposition to war marks him as "a slacker . . . a coward . . . a dirty Red [who] oughta be hanged."[9]

Although the crime for which Peter Owens is ultimately executed is his association with those workers who are opposed to war, it is an association which is very slow to develop. At the outset of the play, a unionized group of longshoremen are refusing to load ships with munitions, and Owens' friend, Walter McCracken, tries to convince him to join the picketing. Peter shrugs off McCracken's suggestion, insisting that he has a deadline on a book and can't spare the time. McCracken persists, and taunts his friend: "Tragic. Five hundred professors of psychology'll probably die if they had to wait another day for that book." He warns Owens that munitions mean war, and something has to be done to stop another war.

Still, Peter refuses to become involved: "I'm a scientist, I'm a psychologist; I'm not a champion of causes ... I just don't think a professor ought to be involved in it."

Peter finally agrees to accompany his friend to a rally; and there, despite his desire to remain uninvolved, he gets into an altercation with the police. McCracken tries to read the Declaration of Independence to a gathering of students and workers but is prevented from doing so by the police. Somewhat bewildered by this, Peter begins to read the Declaration, but he too is stopped, and then is arrested. Because the president of the munitions company, John Andrews, is on the board of trustees of the university at which he teaches, Peter is pressured into dropping the "embarrassing" matter. But, offended by the infringements on his freedom of speech, Peter Owens refuses. Instead, he accompanies McCracken to the strikers' headquarters and then to the dock.

At the dock, Peter watches intently as the scabs and strikers exchange insults. When one of the company officers threatens to blacklist the strikers — "If you men quit on me," he warns them, "I'll have you blacklisted in every goddam port from here to Shanghai. You'll never get another job on a ship as long as you live" — some of the German sailors seem unsure of what to do. But their uncertainty disappears as one of the strikers jumps on a box and yells: "Fellow workers, we call upon you — strike. Strike against war! You're workers like us! Strike with us. Fight with us. Fight against the bosses. Fight against the wars.... The bosses want war because they make money from war. But we don't want war. We say to hell with war. To hell with the bosses. Let them fight their own wars."

The sailors are quick to respond. They surge toward the gangplank and begin to throw the cases of munitions overboard. As the workers sing "solidarity forever," McCracken joins in and takes hold of a case. Suddenly, a shot rings out and McCracken falls to the ground. As Act I ends, Peter Owens is seen bending over the body of his dead friend; the silence on the dock is broken only by the increasing screams of police sirens.

As the second act begins, Owens has gone to the University Faculty Club to confront John Andrews, who is to be given an honorary degree. He tells Andrews that it is criminal for men to convert textile mills into mills manufacturing munitions. But Andrews is disdainful of such an argument: he has a responsibility to the men who are employed in the mills as well as to the people who hold shares in them. Moreover, he insists, "the manufacture of munitions doesn't cause war." Peter tries to argue that without munitions there could not be any war, but Andrews once again brushes him aside: "But they are being manufactured, Owens. If I didn't make 'em someone else would. Why shouldn't I? That's just the way things are." "If that's the way things are," Owens replies angrily, "then perhaps they ought to be changed."

The argument abruptly ends, and Owens asks that the university withhold the honorary degree from the munitions manufacturer. The request is ignored; the faculty is opposed to war, but it is also opposed to the strike because "it's being led by Communists," and Communists are troublemakers. Peter is too politically naive to argue with such a contention. What he does know is that it was Andrews' gunman who killed his friend: "If John Andrews hadn't paid his salary, that gunman wouldn't have killed McCracken." And almost as an afterthought, he adds: "I'm no Communist, and I hold no brief for Communism. But I know this, that if you don't make trouble, you keep quiet, and if you keep quiet, you let things happen — you let war happen."

"Things" happen to Peter Owens, and they happen quickly. First, word of his confrontation with Andrews spreads throughout the university, and Peter suddenly finds himself in the position of being considered the campus Red. Then some intoxicated alumni break into his home singing "Pete Owens is a Red" and try to force him to apologize to Andrews. When he refuses, they decide to lynch him. Now singing "We'll hang Peter Owens to a sour apple tree," they tie his hands and legs and begin to drag him toward the door; only the unexpected return of Pete's wife brings a halt to the merriment as the would-be lynchers shamefacedly disperse. The next day, when Owens and some pickets try to disrupt the commencement exercise (at which Andrews is to receive his honorary degree), the alumni retaliate by shouting, "Throw 'em out. Get those Reds. Throw the dirty Reds out of here. Give it to 'em. Dirty Reds!" A struggle ensues, a shot rings out, someone falls, a voice yells, "Get that son of a bitch Owens," and Act II comes to an end with the police dragging Owens away.

The final act of *Peace on Earth* consists of a series of closely related flashbacks and fantasies, clearly influenced in its technique by the writings of the German Expressionists.[10] War is imminent. Peter Owens is in a cell, waiting to be executed. He still does not believe that another war will be declared: to do so would be sheer folly. But he has no arguments for his cellmate's contention that people go to war simply because they are products of the system: "The system goes to war," he says to Owens, "and they go along with it." Peter's thoughts begin to wander (as the scenes rapidly change) to the Faculty Club, the commencement exercises, and finally to the courtroom in which he was sentenced. His last statement is addressed to the judge who is about to sentence him to death:

I'm innocent. I've committed no crime. I was tried for the murder of William Morris and convicted for something else. You have no right to sentence me for murder because I haven't been found guilty of murder. But if my crime wasn't murder, if my crime was opposition to war, if my crime was association with workers fighting against war, then I am guilty. You can sentence me for those crimes, you can hang me — but you can't stop that fight. For those crimes I'm willing to be sentenced. For those crimes I'm willing to die.

As the speech ends, a chant of "Fight with us, Fight against war, Fight with us, Fight against war" is heard offstage. And it continues to increase in volume as the prison guards take Peter Owens from his cell to be executed.

III *Propaganda to Make One Think*

The critical reaction to *Peace on Earth* was mixed. The Establishment press found the play inferior to "Merry Go Round": Maltz and Sklar may have meant well, John Mason Brown wrote in the *New York Post,* but they have written badly; "they have done nothing more than bring an undergraduate fervor to the repetition of a sermon which every one agrees with in advance."[11] And Brooks Atkinson told his readers that *Peace on Earth* was "hysterically written," a "jumbled, ill-considered propaganda play." Yet, as Atkinson felt "compelled" to conclude his review in *The New York Times,* although he held no brief with the ideas or workmanship of *Peace on Earth,* he "was made furiously to think"; and perhaps, he admitted, "that is all the authors intended."[12] It was just this point, of course, which many left-wing critics singled out for praise. Joseph Freeman, reviewing the play for the *Daily Worker,* called *Peace on Earth* "a landmark in the American theatre"; "it is a continuation," Freeman wrote, "on a higher technical level of the movement, now several years old, to create a drama dealing with the class struggle from a revolutionary viewpoint."[13]

Not all writers who regarded art as a weapon, however, were pleased with *Peace on Earth.* For some, the play was not sufficiently propagandistic. John Howard Lawson, writing in *New Theatre,* spoke of *Peace on Earth* as "a fine achievement" — a genuine beginning of proletarian art in the professional American theater — but he objected to the "muddled" symbolism of the final act, which Lawson felt caused the full impact of the theme, and "the role of the working class in connection with this theme," to be somewhat lost.[14] Similarly, in *New Masses,* William Gardner found much in the play that he liked, but he could not endorse *Peace on Earth* without reservation because there was too much emphasis on Peter Owens's personal sacrifice.[15]

Despite the generally unfavorable reviews which it received in the commercial press, *Peace on Earth* ran for sixteen weeks. That it was able to do so was a personal triumph for the Theatre Union. In part, the respectable run was due to the organization's policy of free ticket distribution to the unemployed, the low cost of tickets in general (of the 1,100 seats at the Civic Repertory Theatre, six hundred were priced from thirty to seventy-five cents), and 158 theater parties.[16] Just as important was the passionate commitment on the part of everyone connected with the organization to bring audiences to see the play. Members of the Executive Board, for example, spoke to community and trade union organizations as often as four times a week, acquainting them with the existence of the Theatre Union, urging them to send representatives to see *Peace on Earth* and informing them of the advantages of theater parties. (And, at the end of each performance of the play, one of the members of the Executive Board would tell the audience that free tickets had been provided for the unemployed and ask those who wished to contribute to this policy; about $100.00 a week was contributed by the audience.[17])

Because of the relative success of *Peace on Earth,* the Theatre Union had no difficulty in raising money for its second production, *Stevedore,* which was so successful that it not only paid back its pre-production cost but left the group with enough money to take *Stevedore* on the road and open its third play, Friedrich Wolf's *Sailors of Cattaro.* Although Wolf's play was not as successful as *Stevedore,* and the Chicago run of the Paul Peters-George Sklar play coincided with one of the worst blizzards and cold periods in the history of the city, the Theatre Union was still in a viable financial position and in 1935 plans were launched for a fourth production, Maltz's *Black Pit.*[18]

IV   *Art and Propaganda*

At least one of the objections made by John Howard Lawson and William Gardner to Maltz's first play for the Theatre Union, *Peace on Earth,* is incontestable: despite its anti-capitalistic position, *Peace on Earth* is not staunchly Marxist (and contrary to the view offered in one study of the left-wing theater, Peter Owens is not converted from political neutrality to Marxian militancy[19]). Like many actual liberal intellectuals of the early 1930s, Owens identifies with the struggle of the proletariat without becoming a Marxist. It may well be, as Gerald Rabkin has suggested in *Drama and Commitment,* that the plays produced by the Theatre Union did not adopt a militantly Marxist position because the Theatre Union could not afford to lose the support of non-Communists.[20] (Its position, as Liston Oak wrote in reply to Lawson's article, was that of a nonsectarian, united front policy.)[21]

Be that as it may, the character of Peter Owens was always conceived by Maltz and Sklar as that of a pacifist; "it was not out of a desire to retain the support of a certain section of our audience," Maltz insists, "that Owens was so characterized."[22] And it is interesting to note that in his second play for the Theatre Union — *Black Pit* — Maltz (this time working without George Sklar's collaboration) again created an unorthodox Marxist situation. His sympathies are as apparent as they were in *Peace on Earth:* capitalism is an evil force which must be fought by the proletariat. But Maltz's artistic sensibility makes such a blatantly propagandist situation much more complex. Not only does he choose a "scab" as his central figure for *Black Pit,* but he portrays him with great sympathy — certainly with much more sympathy than would be compatible with an orthodox Marxist attitude. *Black Pit,* in fact, marked the first serious conflict between Maltz's political and aesthetic sensibilities.

V   Black Pit

Black Pit begins with a brief prologue. The set description is simple: a room with bars. A justice of the peace joins the right hands of Joe Kovarsky and Iola Prescott, and then recites the marriage vows to them. When he is finished, a man walks up to Joe, locks a pair of handcuffs over his wrist, connects the other end to himself, and the two men walk off into the darkness.

Three years later, Joe is released from prison.[23] He had been jailed for taking part in a strike, and was falsely accused of having been a dynamiter; when he returns to his brother-in-law's shabby quarters, he learns that he has been blacklisted (and that Tony, his brother-in-law, has been crippled in an accident). Iola wants Joe to speak to her cousin, Prescott, who is the superintendent of Henrietta Mine 4, but Joe irately refuses: "In blacklist," he tells Iola in his heavy Polish accent, "relation mak' no diff'rence. He no give me job ... I no lak you cousin Prescott. He wan' help me he tell true I no blow oop tipple — but he no tell. He leaves me go prison. I no wan' see him now — I go take odern name, go by Pittsbourg, I t'ink I get job."[24]

Joe does get a job, but when his true identity is discovered he once again finds himself without work. He returns home, and this time he agrees to speak with Prescott. The superintendent offers to put him on the payroll — if he will be an informer for the company: "There's no union here now Joe," he tells him, "except for the company union, and there's not gonna be any ... I want this mine t'stay quiet. If a man doesn't like it here, I wanna know who he is. I don't want any trouble-makers comin' in. That's all I'm askin', boy." At first, Joe refuses to be a stool pigeon. But Iola is due to give birth shortly, and unless Joe is on the company's payroll the doctor won't tend to her. So Joe decides to accept Prescott's offer, without in fact becoming an informer: "Sure, sure, Iola, I can fool heem. Take'm job. Tall heem lil' t'ing no matt'r anybody. Sure ... Sure! Sure, I fool heem. Take'm job. Get Dohctor. Make lil' bit mohney. After while — say g'bye, go away — sure. Man got live lak man, Iola. Man no can live in hole, lak animal!"

Despite his resolve not to become an informer, Joe soon begins to feel the pressure of his new position. His working partner is badly burned in a part of the mine where a gas pocket has built up and the miners want to organize and strike. Prescott learns of the meeting the miners hold and wants Joe to tell him who the organizer is. Joe feigns ignorance, and tells Prescott he has to get the doctor for Iola. "What doctor?" Prescott asks him. "You're fired. You're not working for this company any more. You're not entitled t' the doctor." To Joe's cry of disbelief, Prescott coldly responds: "Tell me the name of the organizer. Joe, so help me Jesus, I'm gonna evict you tomarra morning. I'll take you an' Iola an' the kid an' I'll kick you out on the road an' you'll stay there." So Joe Kovarsky becomes a stool pigeon.

And, of course, it isn't long before the miners discover that Joe has been an informer: "Iola — we say gone get lil' bit sun," Joe cries to his wife, "now sun be black lak night — black lak Pit be. . . ." There is nothing for Joe to do but go away — "go odern place," as Tony tells him, "you be dead man here." Joe does leave, and without Iola and his son; little Tony, Joe tells his wife, must grow up to be a good union man — a man who will fight the company. As Joe leaves the camp, the miners begin their strike, and the play ends with the crippled Tony asserting his faith in the coming of a better world: "Nevair min', Iola . . . . nevair min'! . . . leely feller gone grow oop . . . he no got crawl on belly get piece bread eat . . . outside miner be fight . . . By God, miner gone raise head oop in sun . . . Holler out loud 'Jesus Chris' miner got blow whistle . . . not boss blow . . . miner blow' . . . Jesus Chris' I nevair gone die . . . I gone sit here wait for dat time!' "

VI   *From Drama to Fiction*

The critical response to *Black Pit,* which opened at the Civic Repertory Theatre on March 20, 1935, and ran for eighty-five performances, was divided much more along sectarian lines than had been the case with "Merry Go Round" and *Peace on Earth.*[25] To a critic such as Brooks Atkinson, for example, the chief defect of *Black Pit* was its uncritical use of the stock melodramatic formula: "Although virtue does not win," Atkinson commented, "the villainies of the boss and the helplessness of the victim have a hackneyed look, no matter how earnest the author's intention may be."[26] This view was supported by Joseph Wood Krutch, who wrote in *The Nation* that *Black Pit* "satisfies the requirements of the formula for 'social drama' without accomplishing that something more without which the fulfillment of any formula is rather less than enough."[27] The reaction of Joseph North, on the other hand, who reviewed the play for *New Masses,* was quite different. "When the playwright sets out to tell his audience of workmen that obloquy and limitless misery are the lot of the traitor, he tells a tale more than twice told," North wrote: ". . . if through indirection the tragedy of the stool pigeon would cast into bolder relief the heroism of the rank and file (for that is the greater reality) then Maltz's emphasis could be understood."[28] So it went. The propaganda of *Black Pit* was too severe for the critic of the *New York Times* but too indirect for the reviewer of *New Masses*. On all fronts, *Black Pit* was regarded as the weakest of Maltz's plays.[29]

Maltz himself was not completely satisfied with *Black Pit*. As he was to note rightly years later, "some parts of this play make depressing reading ... I am thinking especially of the sticky moralizing, particularly in the last scene."[30] At the time, however, he was most disappointed in the casting of the play and in the failure of his use of broken-English dialogue (which critics found to be "an impediment in dramatic speech"[31]) as a means of helping the actors. More importantly, he was beginning to find that characterization was easier to develop in fiction than in a play. As a result, *Black Pit* turned out to be his last attempt at a full-length play. In the 1930s he wrote two one-act plays, "Private Hicks" (1935) and "Rehearsal" (1938), as well as a radio play about education, "Red Head Baker" (1937).[32] These, together with a one-act play written in 1952, "The Morrison Case," were Maltz's only other attempts at playwriting.[33] And of these, only "Private Hicks" was of particular significance. An anti-Fascist, anti-war play, "Private Hicks" was first published in *New Theatre;* it received the New Theatre League Prize for the best one-act play against war and Fascism, and in 1939 was reprinted in William Kozlenko's important collection, *The Best Short Plays of the Social Theatre*. But from 1935 on, Maltz's prime artistic concern was with fiction, and until 1940 with the short story in particular.

CHAPTER 3

The Way Things Were

THREE years after the production of *Black Pit,* Maltz published his first collection of stories, *The Way Things Are.*[1] All but one of the eight stories in the collection had been previously published, and at least two of the stories had already attracted considerable attention; "Man on a Road," originally published in *New Masses* in 1935, was included in *The Best Short Stories of 1936,* and "Season of Celebration," first published in *Story* (September, 1937) as "Hotel Raleigh, The Bowery," was reprinted in the Harper-*Story* anthology of novellas, *The Flying Yorkshireman.*

Not all the stories, as one might expect, are of equal merit. But, on the whole, the collection marked an important advance in Maltz's art. His viewpoint continued to be Marxist, and art for Maltz was still a weapon in the class war. But more and more it became apparent, as one critic observed, that "it must be tough on a sensitive artist like Maltz to hew to the party line."[2] It became apparent, that is, that unlike most of the proletarian writers of the 1930s, Maltz's art was capable of transcending the limitations of social proselytizing.

"Merry Go Round" had been the work of two writers just learning their trade, and the play offered little characterization. Much the same was true of *Peace on Earth,* although the characterization of Peter Owens was a perceptible improvement on that of Ed Martin. And Joe Kovarsky was not only a considerably more interesting character than either Ed Martin or Peter Owens, but unlike the bellhop and the college teacher he remains interesting. By not hewing to a strictly party line — by caring as much for his aesthetic concerns as he did for his political alliance — Maltz began to put himself into the tradition of Maxim Gorki (more than one critic at the time considered *The Way Things Are* to be an American *Lower Depths*³). The enormous advance the collection of short stories marked over Maltz's earlier work may be gauged by Alfred Kazin's enthusiastic review in the *New York Herald Tribune:*

Albert Maltz's favorite subject is pain — the appearance of pain, the conditions of pain. Yet it is because he writes out of a hot, lacerating fury that never rises to a scream that these few stories are so burningly effective. He is a good technician, but not an impeccable one; yet the occasional crudity that would ruin another writer is easily passed over. For though he is a humble writer, a taker of notes, the sense of his own anger is the most powerful element in these stories; yet he never enters them visibly. He is rather a witness of the American landscape, a recorder of the break in the dream, of the swelling heartbreak that comes over people struggling with their fingertips against disaster.⁴

The break in the dream, the pain and disaster of which Maltz writes, is of course the failure of the American Dream. And the world of which he writes in *The Way Things Are* is the America of the Great Depression: neither the platitudes of Herbert Hoover nor the New Deal of Franklin Roosevelt made the failure of the Dream any less real. People were starving, and Hoover to the contrary, the country needed something more than "a good, big laugh." A meaningful voice of protest had to be raised, conditions had to be described as they were, and Maltz did just that in *The Way Things Are.*

I *"Season of Celebration"*

The Way Things Are begins with the longest of Maltz's short stories, "Season of Celebration" (which was dramatized by Philip Stevenson and published in *One Act Play Magazine* in October, 1937, under the title, *Transit*). Together with Edward Dahlberg's *Bottom Dogs* and *From Flushing To Calvary,* Nelson Algren's *Somebody in Boots,* and Tom Kromer's *Waiting for Nothing,* it was one of the few works of the 1930s which was concerned with the "bottom dogs" of American society.⁵

The setting for "Season of Celebration" is a Bowery flophouse on New Year's Eve. At nine in the evening, the Hotel Raleigh is virtually empty; only the night man, Bill Benson, and young Jimmy O'Shaughnessy — dying of a ruptured appendix — are to be seen. It isn't very long, though, before old and new inhabitants come stumbling in. Luke Hall, a young innocent from Arkansas, is the first to enter. Unemployed, like most of the people who come to the flophouse, Luke has journeyed to New York to find work, and has come to the Raleigh because he is almost broke and because it's New Year's Eve "and Ah'll be right glad to have company. Ah'm right fond of company."

At first only the dying Jimmy is Luke's company. Then the room begins to fill up and Luke tries to get someone to celebrate with him. But there is nothing to celebrate for a bottom dog: the twisting figure of young O'Shaughnessy makes that clear. "America Waits for Midnight," the headline in the newspaper reads — a happy country was waiting for midnight. But what of Jimmy O'Shaughnessy? And what of himself? thinks Harold Blessy, as he returns to the Raleigh after a day of shoveling snow. "What was he waiting for? Something, but not midnight. Sure, a job, a woman, a home. Christ, everybody was waiting for that. And tired waiting! Your bones were beginning to crack with waiting! O'Shaughnessy was sick from waiting. Free, white and waiting." It's the world of Gorki's *Lower Depths,* to be sure, as it is the world of Harry Hope's bar in Eugene O'Neill's *The Iceman Cometh.* But it is also the world of Tom Kromer's *Waiting for Nothing* and Samuel Beckett's *Waiting for Godot.* Everybody in Room B of the flophouse is waiting; only like Jimmy O'Shaughnessy they have nothing to wait for but death. And while they wait they are overcome with a feeling of weary, lonely desire: "God," thinks Hal Blessy, "what a different New Year's for a guy who had a job and a girl. God, you could go crazy year after year. It had to stop sometime. A man couldn't . . . all the time."

Loneliness and death: the season of celebration is always the same for the bottom dogs of American society; as always, there is nothing to celebrate. Some of the men in the Hotel Raleigh fall asleep, while those who remain awake quarrel and fight with one another. Then, an hour before the New Year, Jimmy O'Shaughnessy lets out a nightmarish scream, and the men in the room become paralyzed with fear. To each man O'Shaughnessy's terrifying cry is the touchstone of his own fear. For a moment, no one is sure who has screamed — himself or another. And as they wait for an ambulance to arrive, each man senses his own death in the anguished throes of the young O'Shaughnessy. Billy Benson, "a seamed, ugly man of fifty," hovers over the dying body and finally blurts out what all the men have been thinking: "Me . . . that's me." In a strange, mournful voice filled with bitterness and defeat, he cries out: "I'm the best goddam harvester mechanic in the whole United States.... I've got a pair of hands that can handle machinery like a goddam, new born baby. But they turned me into a bum.... An' *I* let 'em!" By the time the ambulance arrives, just a few minutes before midnight, Jimmy O'Shaughnessy is dead.

Peritonitis is the official cause of death. To the men in the flophouse, however, the ruptured appendix is a result rather than the cause of Jimmy's death. "He died from not having a job," one of the men screams savagely. "He died 'cause he couldn't eat right an' couldn't live right an' 'cause he didn't have sense enough to fight." But, like Jimmy, most of the men are too weary and despondent to fight. Only Reynolds, a Communist, can think of fighting against the system that has killed Jimmy O'Shaughnessy. As the New Year begins he is seen excitedly explaining to Zets, a pockmarked Russian laborer, why the working class must unite, while Luke Hall, who has taken O'Shaughnessy's coat, softly sings a hymn, then prays — "Oh Jesus, ah need a job bad. You got to give me one before ah die like that poor man heah tonight. You'll help me Jesus, won't you? Please God?" — and finally curls up like a child and goes to sleep, his face still wet with tears.

II   *"Man on a Road"*

Even more impressive than "Season of Celebration" is the concluding story in *The Way Things Are,* "Man on a Road." Originally published in *New Masses,* "Man on a Road" was included in the influential anthology edited by Joseph Freeman, *Proletarian Literature in the United States,*[6] and it remains one of the finest examples of social protest literature to be produced in America. A classic of left-wing writing, it is said to have been reprinted in more trade union and labor papers in the United States than any other story, and reputedly was responsible in some measure for a Congressional investigation into silicosis.[7] As Edward J. O'Brien wrote in *Best Short Stories of 1936,* " 'Man on a Road' is a model of its kind in its emphasis of understatement, full realization of all social implications and simple dignity."[8]

Jack Pickett, a coal miner, discovers that he is dying of rock-dust in his lungs: he has contracted silicosis because the company for which he worked had refused to supply the men with masks or to install a fan system in the tunnels. When he learns that he has only four months to live, Pickett takes to the road so that he won't be a burden to his family. He hitches a ride from the narrator of the story, who describes Pickett as being like "a man in a deep sleep ... [with] eyes that seemed to have a glaze over them." Despite the length of the journey, Pickett says little; the narrator's conversation, the rattle of the car, the steady downpour: they "were all a distant buzz — the meaningless, outside world that could not quite pierce the shell in which [Pickett] seemed to be living."

When they arrive at their destination, Pickett accepts his companion's offer of coffee and a sandwich, and then asks him if he would write a letter to his wife for him. The letter — the crux of the story — reads in part:

The doctor says i hev got me thet sickness like Tom Prescott and thet is the reason wy i am coughin sometime. My lungs is agittin scab like. There is in all ova a hondred men war have this death sickness from the tunel. It is a turible plague becus the doctor says this wud not be so if the company had gave us masks to ware an put a right fan sistem in the tunel.

So i am agoin away becus the doctor says i will be dead in about fore months.

i figger on gettin some work maybe in other parts. i will send you all my money till i caint work no mohr.

i did not want i should be a burdin upon you all at hum. So thet is wy i hev gone away....

i hope you will be well and keep the young one out of the mines. Doan let him work there.

Doan think hard on me for agoin away and doan feel bad. But wen the young one is agrowed up you tell him wat the company has done to me.

i reckon after a bit you shud try to git you anotha man. You are a young woman yit.

Little else happens, little else need happen; the point has been made. As Pickett sits drinking his cup of coffee, the life in his eyes slowly goes out: "It seemed to recede and go deep into the sockets like a flame of a candle going into the night. Over the eyeballs came that dull glaze. I had lost him. He sat deep within himself in his sorrowful, dark absorption." That was all: nothing could be done. "In me there was only mute emotion," the narrator comments; "pity and love for him, and a cold, deep hatred for what had killed him."

III   The Way Things Are

A love for those who are destroyed, and a deep, cold hatred for those who destroy, is the operating sensibility throughout *The Way Things Are;* it is a sensibility which receives its finest artistic presentation in "Season of Celebration," "Man on a Road," and in the title story, "The Way Things Are."[9] With the exception of "Season of Celebration," "The Way Things Are" is the longest story in the collection, and it is the only story that does not deal primarily with the plight of the proletariat. The setting is Louisiana; the conflict is ostensibly between black and white. To be sure, the story has all the earmarks of a standard proletarian work. But the focus of interest for Maltz in neither the too-good-to-be-true Black youth, George Beecher, nor the all-too-true Sheriff Tuckahue; it is, rather, in the confused and bewildered racial attitudes of the white planter, Avery Smallwood.

Smallwood, as his name implies, is a small man with delicate, handsome features. A successful plantation owner, he is dissatisfied with his existence and paints as a refuge from the world of commerce. It is a world of grasp and grab, a world he despises: "There were too many pigs in the world already. He needn't add himself." Smallwood prides himself upon his intellectual and cultural superiority, just as he prides himself upon what he considers to be a benevolent attitude toward his workers. But for all his benevolence, he is still white — still Southern — and he cannot ignore the fact that one of his Black workers broke the jaw of his overseer, Ed Bailey. That young Beecher was trying to prevent Bailey from raping a girl hardly more than ten years old is irrelevant. Indeed Smallwood does not doubt that Beecher had good cause to strike Bailey; but you just "couldn't overlook it when a nigrah hit a white man." No — there was no way out; Beecher had to be punished. But there would be no brutality; there "was going to be no nigrah beating or lynch parties for a boy of his." It had to be handled properly; that's why Smallwood summoned Sheriff Tuckahue to his plantation.

Smallwood and Tuckahue represent opposite ends of the Southern white spectrum; they are, in effect, the Sartorises and Snopeses of Maltz's South. They despise each other, but they also need one another. Tuckahue fears Smallwood's power and wants Bailey's job. Smallwood needs Tuckahue to take some of the starch out of Beecher, for as the planter tells the sheriff: "We just can't let him feel he can raise his hand like that and go free as a sparrow.... For his own good he's got to be taught." Tuckahue wants to "teach" Beecher in his usual fashion: "It ain't the first niggah ah've perked up with a little pistol whupping,'' Tuckahue blurts. "Ah'll better him ovah night." But that is not what Smallwood wants. "Tell you what you do," Smallwood instructs the sheriff. "You take Beecher and set him in the worst cell you got. Don't give him no bed to sleep on. Give him a plate of slop once a day that'll turn his stomach. And just forget about him. Ah reckon after he sits hungry and thirsty for a couple of days, he'll come back here and think it's Paradise. He'll think twice before he hits a white man again. . . ." After a pause he adds earnestly, "You know, ah don't like to do this . . . But it's sure for the boy's own good. He don't learn now, he'll learn it bitter some other day. That's true, ain't it?"

Although he is afraid to say anything, Tuckahue is outraged by Smallwood's attitude. And he becomes even more incensed when he learns that George Beecher will not apologize for breaking the jaw of the overseer. Smallwood wants the young Black to say he is sorry; instead, Beecher fiercely asserts the justice of his act: "Nossuh! Ah do it again. Niggah get lynched for what Bailey done!" Tuckahue is astounded by Beecher's "arrogance" and warns the youth that "Niggah get lynched for what you do . . . What's the matter with you, boy, talkin' like that? What you do, an' what a white man does, is two hell of a different things. An' don't you evah forget it!" But Beecher persists in defending himself, and when an exasperated Smallwood tells him that he will personally "tend" to the injured overseer, Beecher screams at him in a voice filled with scorn and bitterness, "You talk sweet but you *do* like all the rest! You gone put me on a chain gang but *he* ain't gone be there! You *know* he ain't! *You just lyin'!*"

Instinctively, Smallwood slaps Beecher across the face. Then — slowly — he realizes that he has been lying: a look of strange, wild shame passes over his face as he recognizes that "a nigrah boy had showed him for a liar." To Tuckahue's amazement, and to his own chagrin, Smallwood turns to Beecher and in a low voice apologizes for hitting him and promises to dismiss Bailey. Yet his very next sentence makes clear how strong his white Southern ties are: "But you, George, you can't hit a white man an' not suffer for it . . . Ah'm sorry, George, but you've got to learn that. You've got to learn what this world's like we live in. If you don't learn, you'll end up on the limb of a tree. Ah wouldn't want that happening to you."

Tuckahue and his deputy put Beecher on the floor of their car, cover him with a mule blanket, and begin to drive back to town. As the deputy drives, Tuckahue drinks cheap whiskey. The more he drinks, the more vicious he becomes; and before long, George Beecher becomes the natural outlet for his frustration. To frighten Beecher, the sheriff pretends that a lynch party is following the car. He taunts his prisoner, and tells him to "Think of something, boy! Don't think of the lynchin'! They ain't gonna get you. They said they was goin' t' tie you to the back of a car — drag you till you scraped to death — but they ain't agonna do that, boy. Think of something!" He then orders the deputy to slow down the car, and as he does Beecher leaps to his feet and flings himself out of the car.

Later that day Smallwood receives word that George Beecher had tried to escape from Sheriff Tuckahue and was lying on the road with his head crushed. Saddened, feeling slightly nauseous, Smallwood sits with his head gripped with both hands and thinks: "A man just had to make himself hard, and then try to forget about it." To forget about it, really for want of something to do, Avery Smallwood, the well-meaning, paternalistic planter, starts to clean his paint brushes.

IV   *"The Game"*

The remaining five stories in *The Way Things Are* are lesser achievements than "Season of Celebration," "Man on a Road," and "The Way Things Are," but they are by no means unsuccessful stories. In "The Game,"[10] a father teaches his young son how to steal a bottle of milk: to the boy, it's a game; to the father, it's a matter of survival. The boy assures his father that he won't grow up to be a thief; he knows that stealing is wrong. What the boy wants is to grow up to be as strong as his father and to get a job. But the father knows better; his son will never be very strong: "When I was your age," he says to himself, "I was a head taller than you. You poor little monkey, they're not giving you a chance to grow up."

The frustration and loneliness of the father are punctuated more by his silence than by what he says. This is equally true of the central figures in "Good-by" and "The Drop-Forge Man."[11] Indeed, not unlike the silences in Hemingway's stories, the silences in *The Way Things Are* are as significant as anything that is said. In "Good-by," for example, a young girl attends the funeral of her father and decides that she must leave home; she can no longer tolerate the conditions that have killed her father and that are slowly causing her brother to go deaf from years of working in a nail factory. But there is no meaningful way for her to articulate her frustration. As the bus leaves the town, she sees the Bessemer furnace lighting the sky, the mill, the town itself, in a blaze of red, and in a convulsive, almost choking sob, can only cry out, "Good-by you bastard . . . good-by you bastard."

So, too, Leeman Hayes, the drop-forge man, finds it impossible to express the anguish of operating a steam hammer, and the loneliness of sharing a room with his cousin Bob and Bob's wife, Ella. His sexual frustration leads him to a gypsy fortune teller, who takes his money and, to Leeman's dismay, will only tell his fortune. Angry, Leeman stands on a street corner and curses the gypsy, his job, his cousin, and himself: "He prayed to God to make things different for him, to give his father some money, to let him go home, to give him a girl who would walk down the street on his arm." He falls to the sidewalk, feeling nothing but "his pounding heart, like the pound-pound of his terrible drop-forge"; rubbing his forehead on the damp stone, he lies quietly at last, listening to "the steam hammer beating at him, beating monotonously, terribly like a pulse in his heart."

V   *"Incident on a Street Corner"*

"Incident on a Street Corner"[12] and "A Letter from the Country"[13] differ from the other stories in *The Way Things Are* to the extent that they offer little or no character portrayal. In both stories a group of men stand in opposition to the forces of corrupt America: in "Incident on a Street Corner" the corruption is represented by two policemen, and in "A Letter from the Country" it is represented by union breakers. The two stories are the weakest in the collection.

The "incident" on the street corner arises from an attempt by two policemen to arrest a young drunk. A crowd quickly gathers, and it watches as the police struggle futilely to get the man to go with them. When he finally falls to his knees, one of the policemen smashes his knee into the man's nose, breaking it. As blood starts to gush from the nose, the already hostile but silent crowd begins to express its hatred for the police. Exasperated, the older of the two policemen turns to the crowd and says bitterly: "You talk like we was apes or something . . . I'm an Irishman, an' a Catholic. I've got my dooty as I do it." An angry response comes from a middle-aged man: "I'll tell you somethin', brother — as one Irishman to another: it was a good Catholic like you who cracked my skull in the dock strike of nineteen-fourteen. When an Irish-Catholic puts on a cop's uniform, he's a cop. He's no Irishman or Catholic any longer." The rest is silence. When the younger policeman blurts out nervously, "What's the matter with you? What the hell's the matter with you?" there is no reply; the people simply stand in the rain and wait for the ambulance; there is nothing more to be said between them and the police.

The need for a united proletariat, which is implicit in "Incident on a Street Corner," becomes the very essence of "A Letter from the Country." The story — though it is more tract than story — is in the form of a letter from a farmer, Lester Cooley, to a friend in the city. Cooley tells his friend how he and several other union organizers had been beaten and humiliated by a group of anti-union people, and asks his friend if he would write about the incident for his magazine — "to let people know concerning some of the things that is happening in this good old U.S.A." None of the local newspapers would print a word about the incident, the town sheriff had himself been one of the culprits, and the governor had replied to a demand that action be taken by stating that it was out of his jurisdiction. "How do you like that?" Cooley asks rhetorically. "I guess we sure are dirt farmers all right. Dirt to him." But Cooley takes solace in the fact that "it learned us all a great deal ... it just shows [Cooley concludes] that we farmers have got to make our union like the thistle out here, that never stops growing no matter how hard you try to get rid of it. Not good to look at, but hard to down."

VI   *"The Happiest Man"*

If "Incident on a Street Corner" and "A Letter from the Country" are perhaps Maltz's weakest stories, "The Happiest Man on Earth" is certainly his finest. First published in the June, 1938, issue of *Harper's* magazine,[14] it won the O. Henry Memorial Award as the best short story for that year (second and third prizes went to Richard Wright's "Fire and Cloud" and John Steinbeck's "The Prize"). That "The Happiest Man on Earth" suffered from none of the proselytizing pitfalls that marred "Incident on a Street Corner" and "A Letter from the Country" is implicit not only in the prize it was awarded by such Establishment jurors as Harry Hansen, Irita Van Doren, Fred T. Marsh, and Edward Weeks, but also in the praise it received from the bourgeois press: "The Happiest Man on Earth," Ruth Bower wrote in the Sunday *Tribune* on November 6, 1938, "has the particular and immediate effectiveness of art that is lacking in the essentially inartistic techniques of realistic reporting of enraged propaganda, which have been the vehicle of much proletarian writing in the past."

The happiest man on earth is Jesse Fulton, a linotyper who has been out of work for six years. When he learns that his brother-in-law, Tom Brackett, is in charge of the trucking department of an oil company in Oklahoma, he walks from Kansas City to Tulsa with one thought sustaining him throughout the grueling trip: before long he will once again have work to do. But to his dismay, Tom refuses to give him a job: "It ain't dynamite you drive," he tells Jesse. "They don't use anything as safe as dynamite in drilling oil wells. They wish they could, but they can't. It's nitroglycerin! Soup!" Jesse doesn't care; it doesn't matter to him that every year one out of five drivers is killed; what matters is that his family is starving and the company pays a dollar a mile.

Tom is still reluctant. He offers to lend Jesse money and tells him that he must have some courage, that he must keep up hope. Jesse refuses the offer and tells his brother-in-law: "I got all the courage you want, but no, I ain't got no hope. The hope was dried up in me in six years' waiting. You're the only hope I got." Tom warns him that if he drives one of the trucks the only certain thing is that "sooner or later you get killed." Jesse won't be put off: "Okay, then," he shouts at Tom. "Then I do. But meanwhile I got something, don't I. I can buy a pair of shoes. Look at me! I can buy a suit that don't say 'Relief' by the way it fits. I can smoke cigarettes. I can buy some candy for the kids. I can eat some myself. Yes, by God, I want to eat some candy. I want a glass of beer once a day. I want Ella dressed up. I want her to eat meat three times a week, four times maybe. I want to take my family to the movies." Tom gives in and tells Jesse that he can drive that evening. Despite the danger, and with eyes still glistening with tears, Jesse's gaunt face begins to shine with a kind of fierce radiance. "I'm the happiest man in the world," he whispers to himself. "I'm the happiest man on the whole earth."

"The Happiest Man on Earth" is a powerful and finely wrought story, perhaps the single most impressive piece of writing Maltz has done. It well deserved the O. Henry award, and together with the stories in *The Way Things Are* more than justifies Michael Gold's comment that Maltz's stories are written with such a deep and brooding pain that Maltz may well be regarded as "a nerve along which crept all the vast sufferings of the poor."[15]

CHAPTER 4

We Hold These Truths

SHORTLY before the publication of *The Way Things Are* and "The Happiest Man on Earth," Maltz became associated with a group of people who were determined to fight the wave of anti-Semitism — and racism in general — which had been building up in the United States for several years. By 1938, William Dudley Pelley, Fritz Kuhn, Gerald L. K. Smith, and Huey Long had become familiar proponents of American bigotry; none, however, quite attained the following of Father Charles E. Coughlin, the renowned radio priest of the Depression.[1]

Coughlin began his broadcasts in 1926, and at first concerned himself primarily with theological matters. But before very long he decided that "things were slipping away from man's purpose,"[2] and started to devote an increasing amount of attention to politics. His original support of Roosevelt and the New Deal gave way to vicious attacks: Roosevelt was denounced as a "great liar and betrayer" and the New Deal as a huge monster with one foot stuck in "the red mud of Soviet communism, and the other, in the stinking cesspool of pagan plutocracy."[3] As his disenchantment continued, Coughlin joined with Smith and Long in forming the National Union for Social Justice, an ultra-conservative political party. By the mid-thirties, Coughlin purportedly had a radio audience of more than forty million people.[4]

In the first half of the 1930s, Father Coughlin's speeches and writings tended to be populist and progressive (rather than fascist) in ideology. In his radio address of November 11, 1934, in which he set forth "The Principles of the National Union for Social Justice," Coughlin expressed his belief in "a just, living, annual

45

wage" for all who are willing to work; in the right to maintain private property; in "liberty of conscience and liberty of education"; in the right of the laboring man to organize in unions.[5] This is indeed a rhetoric, as James Shenton has commented, which must have had a familiar ring to American audiences.[6]

What undermined Coughlin was his repeated attacks on Roosevelt and the New Deal. The Roman Catholic hierarchy was a strong supporter of Roosevelt, and its dissatisfaction with the "radio priest" grew as his denunciations of the President came to be regarded as the official view of the Catholic Church itself. A year after Roosevelt's overwhelming victory in 1936, and the virtual collapse of Coughlin's Union Party, the late Edward Cardinal Mooney, then the archbishop of Detroit, ordered Coughlin to submit his talks for prebroadcast examination. The board of censors quickly made Coughlin's radio speeches less offensive, but they had no control over his magazine, *Social Justice,* which continued to become increasingly anti-Semitic and pro-Fascist.

Indeed, so blatant and virulent had anti-Semitism become in the United States toward the end of the 1930s that The League of American Writers — "the first child" of The American Writers' Congress, as Waldo Frank called the League[7] — felt compelled to publish a pamphlet entitled *We Hold These Truths,* in which fifty-four prominent figures (including Ruth Benedict, Van Wyck Brooks, Thomas E. Dewey, Theodore Dreiser, Langston Hughes, Tom Mooney, Upton Sinclair, and Dorothy Thompson) denounced the upsurge of anti-Semitism. Maltz's contribution to *We Hold These Truths* included a brief statement as well as the unsigned nine-page introduction to the pamphlet.

The introduction was both an analysis of the phenomenon of anti-Semitism and a call to all concerned people to combat it: "We believe [Maltz wrote] that anti-Semitism is of burning concern to everyone, non-Jew as well as Jew. We believe that silence on this matter will serve only those who wish to destroy democracy. In the presence of injustice, silence is either cowardly or criminal; at best it is impotent, for the vicious do not lie down with the meek, they trample upon them."[8] Two months after the publication of *We Hold These Truths,* Maltz once again had a chance to call for the support of those who opposed anti-Semitism. This time, the occasion was the issuance of the first number of *Equality,* a monthly journal to "Defend Democratic Rights and Combat Anti-Semitism and Racism."[9]

I   Equality

Equality was organized expressly to counteract Father Coughlin's *Social Justice*. It was not only the contents of the magazine but the very way in which it was sold that brought about the formation of *Equality*. By 1938–1939 the so-called Christian Front was selling *Social Justice* on street corners in New York and frequently held anti-Semitic demonstrations in Jewish neighborhoods. The results were usually ugly and violent. James Wechsler, writing for *The Nation* in July, 1939, commented on what he called the rise of "The Coughlin Terror"; "For six months [Wechsler wrote] New York has been somewhat incredulously watching the evolution of an anti-Semitic movement. It is not the polite kind to which most cities are accustomed; its manifestations are angry and violent, it uses the streets as a battleground and it employs all the familiar devices of an ancient crusade. Its spirited leader is Charles E. Coughlin and its book of revelations is his magazine *Social Justice*."[10] *Equality* met the challenge of the Christian Front by hiring a rather large number of unemployed workers to sell the journal (on a commission basis) alongside the salesmen of *Social Justice*. As a result, *Equality* quickly became, in Wechsler's words, "the symbol of the forces with which Coughlinism had to contend."[11]

Although many members of *Equality's* editorial board were Jewish, as were the magazine's initial financial backers, *Equality* was not a Jewish magazine. People of various religious beliefs were affiliated with the magazine, and no attempt was made to espouse the tenets of the Jewish religion; *Equality* was concerned with anti-Semitism rather than Judaism. No doubt in an attempt to attract a wide audience, the editorial masthead included the names of such well-known writers as Moss Hart, Lillian Hellman, and Dorothy Parker — all of whom made financial contributions to *Equality* but were not involved in the actual workings of the journal. For the most part, that was done by Rabbi Michael Alper, Nathan Ausubel, Harold Coy, Albert Deutsch, and Albert Maltz.

Maltz contributed only three signed pieces to *Equality:* two were reviews of novels — John Steinbeck's *Grapes of Wrath* and Richard Wright's *Native Son* — and one was a review of the film, *Gone with the Wind,* which Maltz assailed as "a Bourbon's history of the Civil War."[12] In addition to these signed reviews, however, Maltz also wrote several unsigned pieces, the most important of which was the editorial in the first issue of May, 1939, entitled "To All People of Good Will." Like his introduction to *We Hold These*

Truths, Maltz's editorial condemned those who ignored the rising tide of anti-Semitism, and begged that the lesson of Europe be learned by all Americans: *"That where anti-Semitism triumphs, Fascism triumphs as well.* Fascism and anti-Semitism are indissoluble. They are, and will be, equally indissoluble in America." For this reason, Maltz wrote, *Equality* was being launched. Fascism had become state power in half of Europe, and *Equality* was dedicating itself "to an uncompromising fight against anti-Semitism and racism."

Equality lasted for a year and a half. (Its final number was October-November, 1940.) After the outbreak of World War II in Europe, subscriptions and newspaper sales began to decline rapidly; by 1940, most issues sold less than a thousand copies. The printer went unpaid, and so did the staff. According to Harold Coy, then managing editor of *Equality,* "Many who might have helped in other circumstances were now concerned with all-out aid to Britain and had little patience with a medium that limited itself to its original program of defending the rights of minorities."[13] It was also a time of repressive legislation, of the Smith Act in particular, hardly a propitious time, as Coy notes, "to rally massive support under the banner of equality." And so *Equality* faded away — though some of its participants, particularly Louis Harap, became associated with *Jewish Survey.* Short-lived and uneven in quality as it may have been, *Equality* more than fulfilled its purpose. It not only blunted the militant tactics of the Christian Front; it also played a significant part in both the Church's and the federal government's forcing Coughlin to cease publication of *Social Justice.* Indeed, the silencing in 1941–1942 of the demagogue from the Shrine of the Holy Flower in Royal Oak, Michigan, was a singular if somewhat belated triumph for the staff of *Equality.*

II   *Dissolution of the Left*

The events surrounding the start of World War II made the times unpropitious not only for a journal such as *Equality* but for the literary and intellectual Left in general. With the onset of the Depression, "proletarian" literature had become an important aspect of American literature; but it remained a viable literature only so long as the Depression provided the Left with a stark subject for protest. When the war brought the Depression to an end, it also brought with it the end of the literary movement which had grown out of the

Depression. The events surrounding the war — in particular, the shifting alliances of the Soviet Union — had disillusioned many Communist Party members and fellow travelers, while the war itself deprived the writers on the Left of much of their former subject matter.[14] As a result, there was a movement away from social causes toward an introspective examination of the self, and by 1940 a literature which for almost a decade had been dominated by the Left gave way to works written under the aegis of the New Critics.

III   *A Proletarian Renaissance*

Proletarian literature — the literature of social protest produced by the Left — flourished in the United States from 1930 to 1937.[15] Michael Gold's *Jews Without Money,* Edward Dahlberg's *Bottom Dogs,* Edwin Seaver's *The Company,* and Mary Heaton Vorse's *Strike!* all appeared in the first year of the Depression decade. Succeeding years saw the publication of such classics of left-wing fiction as Grace Lumpkin's *To Make My Bread* (1932), Jack Conroy's *The Disinherited* (1933), Robert Cantwell's *The Land of Plenty* (1934), Edward Newhouse's *You Can't Sleep Here* (1934), William Rollins, Jr.'s *The Shadow Before* (1934), Tom Kromer's *Waiting for Nothing* (1935), Clara Weatherwax's *Marching! Marching!* (1935), Isidor Schneider's *From the Kingdom of Necessity* (1935), Leane Zugsmith's *A Time to Remember* (1936), and Albert Halper's *The Chute* (1937). It was during this period, too, that James T. Farrell's Studs Lonigan trilogy was published, as were the first two novels in Josephine Herbst's trilogy of middle class life.[16] Left-wing "little magazines" also proliferated during this time, and in the pages of such journals as *Partisan Review, Dynamo,* and *The Rebel Poet* one could find the poems of Kenneth Fearing, Sol Funaroff, Horace Gregory, Alfred Hayes, H. H. Lewis, Edwin Rolfe, and Muriel Rukeyser (while *Blast* and *Anvil* devoted themselves to "stories for workers").

The most productive years for the literary Left were 1934 and 1935; and, perhaps not coincidentally, they were also the years in which *Partisan Review* and The League of American Writers were formed. The history of both organizations reflects the changing literary (and political) concerns of the time. In its first issue, the editors of *Partisan Review* proclaimed their intention to concentrate on creative and critical literature; but, they added, "we shall maintain a definite point of view — that of a revolutionary working class."[17] Similarly, Waldo Frank wrote of the first Congress of American Writers: "Traits of the Congress were heartiness, intellectual solidity and, above all, youth. Its principal achievement was, perhaps, to integrate elements and forces of American cultural life which, heretofore, have been anarchic, into the beginning of a literary movement, both broad and deep, which springs from an alliance of writers and artists with the working class."[18]

The call for a Writers' Congress was originally issued so that a League of American Writers might be formed. The League was to be an affiliate of the International Union of Revolutionary Writers and was to be concerned with two particular problems: (1) how the writers on the Left might best face the dangers of war and Fascism; and (2) how they might best present in their work "the fresh understanding of the American scene that has come from [their] enrollment in the revolutionary cause."[19] The Congress was held in April, 1935, and was a great success. Papers were read by James T. Farrell, Edward Dahlberg, Malcolm Cowley, Granville Hicks and Langston Hughes (among others); Waldo Frank was elected chairman of the League; and an Executive Committee of eighteen prominent writers — including Harold Clurman, Joseph Freeman, Josephine Herbst, Matthew Josephson, and Albert Maltz — was elected.

Three more Congresses were held (in 1937, 1939, and 1941), but none attained the success of the first one. In an attempt to establish a united front, the League gave precedence to such "middle ground" writers as Ernest Hemingway and Thornton Wilder at the expense of the Mike Golds and Granville Hickses. At the same time, the affiliation between the League and Waldo Frank had become tenuous at best, and James Farrell, who was generally regarded as the most promising of the young left-wing writers, categorically refused to attend the second Congress. Farrell felt that the writers on the Left not only had no knowledge of dialectic materialism but that the whole left-wing cultural movement was bankrupt. And, as was typical of him, Farrell did not hesitate to express his contempt for those "revolutionary extremists [who] have preached their one-sided functionalism under the banner of 'Marxism' and 'Marxist-Leninism.' "[20] Such disdainful pronouncements quickly brought to a head a long-standing feud between the forces of *Partisan Review* and those of *New Masses* which, in effect, proved to be the death-knell of the literary Left.

IV   *A Partisan Matter*

From its inception, the editorial policy of *Partisan Review* had been more demanding than that of any other left-wing journal. It too accepted the dictum that art was a weapon in the class war; and perhaps the editors of *Partisan Review,* like *New Masses'* Mike Gold, hoped to find a Shakespeare in overalls. But if they did, they did not regard every person in overalls as a Shakespeare. Unlike most of the literature which appeared in *New Masses,* the artistic quality of the stories and poems which were published in *Partisan Review* was remarkably good.

One of the mainstays of *Partisan Review* in its formative years was James Farrell, who contributed stories and essays to the new periodical and for a while even served as its drama critic. In this latter capacity Farrell reviewed (in the February, 1936, issue of *Partisan Review-Anvil*) Clifford Odets' *Paradise Lost,* which he summarily dismissed as a pompous work filled with "dull speeches and swaggering platitudes."[21] It was this review that brought to a boil the feud between *Partisan Review* and *New Masses.* Michael Gold immediately denounced Farrell for his "slaughter" of Odets' play, and condemned the editors of *Partisan Review* for carrying their Marxian scholarship "as though it were a heavy cross."[22] The situation was considerably exacerbated when, later that year, Farrell's *A Note on Literary Criticism* was published. For it was in this volume that Farrell cogently argued that most Marxist critics — including those on *New Masses* — did not understand dialectic materialism; their Marxism, he contended, was based on a profound ignorance of Marx's writings.

In response, the orthodox Left savagely refuted Farrell's work; and, following Granville Hicks' lead, they questioned whether there was anything at all in *A Note on Literary Criticism* that was worth while. (At the same time, Alan Calmer was defending Farrell in the pages of *Partisan Review,* while in his review for *The Nation* Edmund Wilson wrote that Farrell's new work contained one of the "few intelligent discussions of literature from the Marxist point of view which has yet been written by Americans.")[23]

V   *Professional Optimism*

The feud between *Partisan Review* and *New Masses* was not restricted to literary matters. Indeed, by the end of 1936 literary

issues had become quite secondary to political differences. Because it had adopted the Communist Party's 1935 position of a United Front, *New Masses* showed little interest in pursuing its call for a truly proletarian literature; and by December, 1936, William Phillips, anticipating Farrell's barb to the Second Writers' Congress, was already asking readers of *New Masses:* "Have all our critical guarantees that proletarian literature would expand and mature to the point dominating American literature been just so much professional optimism?"[24]

Equally significant was the refusal of the *Partisan* editors to unite the journal with The League of American Writers. For various reasons (many of which were financial), the editors of *Partisan Review* decided to suspend publication in October, 1936. A proposal was then made to have *Partisan Review* become an official affiliate of The League of American Writers, which in turn would help raise money to pay off the journal's outstanding debts. But the editors, William Phillips and Philip Rahv, refused what was clearly a tempting offer. Not only were they convinced that the cultural revolution was a failure; even more, they believed, the Moscow trials and the Spanish Civil War called into serious question their allegiance to the Soviet Union and the Communist Party.[25] By the time *Partisan* was revived in December, 1937, its editors (who now included Fred Dupee, Dwight Macdonald, and Mary McCarthy) had become independent radicals whose political allegiance was to Leon Trotsky. *Partisan Review* clearly had become the voice of opposition: "*Partisan Review* is aware of its responsibility to the revolutionary movement in general," the editors wrote, "but we disclaim obligation to any of its organized political expressions. Indeed, we think that the cause of revolutionary literature is best served by a policy of no commitments to any political party."[26] The new *Partisan,* Fred Dupee commented, would aspire "to represent a new and dissident generation in American letters."[27]

VI   *Writers and Partisans*

Although the Moscow trials caused a severe schism among left-wing intellectuals, they did not destroy the Left. To be sure, to people like Rahv, Phillips, Farrell, and Dwight Macdonald, the trials raised serious questions about the integrity of the Soviet system. For, as James Gilbert observed in his study, *Writers and Partisans; A History of Literary Radicalism in America,* if the Moscow trials were unjust, not only might the struggle for Spain be useless; it might even prove to be a fight "to preserve a government dominated by the same deformed revolutionary spirit that ruled the Soviet state."[28] This possibility notwithstanding, most Party members and fellow travelers managed to justify the trials. But the invasion of Finland and the signing of the Stalin-Hitler pact in 1939 made it increasingly difficult to defend the Soviet Union's supposed anti-Fascist policies. The position of many members of the literary Left was summed up in Granville Hicks' announced resignation from the Communist Party. "There was nothing wrong," Hicks wrote in *The New Republic* on September 9, 1940, "in our belief that the world had to be changed and that we could help to change it." But because the Communist Party now expected him to accept all policies without question, Hicks felt compelled to resign his membership in the Party because it "is no longer an organization in which I can be effective."[29]

Three years later, The League of American Writers was officially disbanded. In point of fact, however, after the signing of the Stalin-Hitler pact only a few members of the literary Left were able to justify the actions of, and actively retain their belief in the eventual success of, the Soviet Union. Michael Gold was one such writer, as were Howard Fast, John North, Isidor Schneider, Dalton Trumbo, and Albert Maltz. Trumbo published his remarkable anti-war *tour de force, Johnny Got His Gun,* in 1939, the same year in which John Steinbeck published *Grapes of Wrath* and a year before the publication of Richard Wright's *Native Son.* Wright and Steinbeck, of course, had been runners-up to Maltz in the 1938 O. Henry Short Story awards; and by a strange quirk of publishing history, in June, 1940, Maltz followed the publication of their most important novels with his most ambitious work to the date, *The Underground Stream.* It was, in many ways, a remarkable publishing event, for while many members of the Left had suddenly turned apologist, *The Underground Stream* was not only written out of a very obvious faith in the Communist Party, but it argued, and argued with a power that far surpassed that of most social novels, that Fascism in the United States could only be defeated by the "underground stream" in American life — the Communist Party.

CHAPTER 5

A Moment in an American Winter

MALTZ called *The Underground Stream* "an historical novel of
a moment in the American winter." The winter was that of
February, 1936; the moment, the attempt to unionize the automotive industry in Detroit. It was a time, as one critic has written,
when "the tension of two social wills, one toward unionization, the
other toward a frank and brutal Fascism, rocked the city
unforgettably."[1]

Certainly there were few developments during the New Deal that
were as far-reaching as the formation of powerful labor unions. By
the mid-thirties, the unions had brought the work week down by
about nine hours from what it had been in 1929; a five- rather than
a six-day work week was becoming common practice; and, at least
in the big cities, shops and factories were closing on Saturday.
Socially and politically, the union became a significant force in
American life.[2] And unlike the role adopted by unions today,
unions in the 1930s represented the most liberal and reform-minded
elements in the United States.

I *Sitting Down*

In the automotive industry, the major reforms were brought
about by the newly organized Committee for Industrial Organization. (So fearful of unionization was the management of General
Motors that between 1934 and 1936 it spent an estimated one million dollars for private detectives in an attempt to ferret out union
organizers.) An offshoot of the American Federation of Labor, the
CIO was organized in November, 1935, at the instigation of John
L. Lewis, head of the United Mine Workers. Lewis felt that the

craft structure of the A. F. of L. hindered the union's growth, and he wanted it replaced with a union of industrial forces. In August, 1935, a start was made with the chartering of the United Automobile Workers and three months later the CIO was formed within the American Federation of Labor.

The most effective weapon to be employed by the CIO was the sit-down strike. It was by no means a new technique: the sit-down had been attempted, with some success, in 1933 by workers of the Horner Packing Company in Minnesota, by Goodyear employees in Akron in 1935, and was being used rather widely in France. But nowhere had it had the intensity and starkness that the CIO brought to it in their sit-down strikes against the automotive industry in 1936–1937. At issue in these strikes was not only wages but the right to union organization with management's recognition of the United Automobile Workers as the sole bargaining agent.

Despite John L. Lewis's fear that a strike against General Motors would ruin the CIO before it really had time to gain power, workers in the Fleetwood and Cadillac plants in Detroit, and in the Fisher plants in Cleveland and Flint, Michigan, went on strike. It began in November, 1936, with a sit-down in Flint, and it was this strike in particular that attracted worldwide attention. For almost two months little happened at the Fisher plants: the workers occupied the factories, while the Governor of Michigan, Frank Murphy, and Secretary of Labor Frances Perkins tried to convince the management of General Motors to negotiate with the United Automobile Workers. Their arguments were to no avail. On January 11, General Motors turned off the heat in Fisher plant no. 2 and ordered the police to prevent food from being sent in to the strikers. Hours later the police rushed the building but were repulsed by the workers. The National Guard was then called to the plant but was ordered not to attack. Labor and management were at a standstill.

Shortly thereafter, General Motors obtained a court writ ordering the workers to evacuate the buildings by the afternoon of February 3 or face imprisonment and a $15,000,000 fine. The workers refused to move; instead, their ranks were solidified by sympathizers from other cities. Then, just as another bloody battle seemed inevitable, Governor Murphy sent word that the management of General Motors had agreed to confer with the United Automobile Workers. Within a week, the labor organization won recognition as the bargaining agent in seventeen G.M. plants and reached an agreement to negotiate a new contract. After forty-four days, the sit-down strike came to an end.

II *Bodies by Fisher*

Maltz was among the many people who went to Detroit and Flint to witness the struggle between labor and management. He arrived in time to see the battle between the police and the strikers in Flint, and reported on the events for *New Masses:*

After ten days of sitting down [Maltz wrote in an article entitled "Bodies by Fisher"] the strikers were without heat or food — and ten days and nights are a long time to be shut up away from home and family with a vicious press to read and a vicious radio to listen to, with stool-pigeons, provocateurs, paid company whisperers, and with the whole uncertainty of the struggle at work to break down morale. Their morale was not broken. At the end of ten days they faced a fight, they fought it out, and today they are flaming with a spirit of solidarity which is much greater than they have had before.[3]

"Bodies by Fisher" notwithstanding, Maltz did not go to Michigan to report on the sit-down strikes. The struggle in the United States for industrial unions seemed to him to have all the dramatic elements requisite for an exciting novel. Not only was his imagination attracted by the personal dangers facing a worker who joined a union in most industries (blacklistings and beatings were common fates for such workers, and murder was not unheard of), but the crucial role played by Communist organizers in the formation of the CIO was equally attractive to his political sensibility. The situation, in short, seemed to Maltz to provide an ideal subject for his first attempt at a novel, and it was primarily to gather material for his new work that he journeyed from New York to Michigan.

III *The Black Legion*

As it turned out, Maltz did not make use of the strikes themselves in *The Underground Stream.* (The time of the novel is set shortly before the actual strikes broke out.) What came to preoccupy his attention even more than the sit-down strikes, and what consequently became the focus of the novel, was the struggle between the Communists who wanted to organize the unions and the incipient Fascist forces of management which tried to destroy both the unions and their organizers.

Maltz of course had gone to Michigan as a very biased observer. And during his stay he became more sympathetic than ever toward the work done by the Communist organizers. For it was only after he arrived in Michigan that Maltz became aware of the enormous power of the forces that were opposing the unionization of labor. Here he first learned of the activities of the Black Legion, a group of white men in Detroit who (starting in 1936) tried to revive the terrorism of the Ku Klux Klan.[4] The Legion, Maltz was informed, frequently was directed by the large automotive companies in an attempt to prevent the organization of labor unions, and in typical Klan fashion would whip, bomb, and, on occasion, shoot union organizers. (It was the Black Legion, Maltz was told, who purportedly had been responsible for the death of Marchuck, one of the best Communist organizers.)

While in Flint, Maltz was also given generally unknown information about two men. One was the head of the Michigan State Police; the other was Harry Bennett, then head of the Ford Motor Company's spy system: Jeffrey Grebb, a major figure in *The Underground Stream,* was a composite of these two men. But, as important as all this newly-gained information was to the composition of *The Underground Stream,* there was a personal preoccupation which was perhaps more important than any other factor in the writing of the novel. "How does a man face death for his principles, how would I face it if I had to?" Maltz wrote some years later in an attempt to recall the wellsprings for his first novel. "This personal aspect was not romantic. Although I was not a trade union, or a Communist organizer, many men like myself had had to face this decision in Nazi Germany. We in the U.S. at that time had to face the possible triumph of the many Fascist forces at work in the U.S." Thus, as would be the case with his next novel, *The Cross and the Arrow, The Underground Stream* may be "political on the surface," but to Maltz its "motor power is supplied by a moral quest."[5]

IV   The Underground Stream

The political aspect of *The Underground Stream* dominates most of the novel, which has an almost contrapuntal structure. Maltz keeps shifting the scene, only he shifts not so much from character to character as from Fascist to Communist and back again. A close look at the first six sections of Part I (the book is divided into three parts) makes the novel's structure, and Maltz's political intent, quite clear.

Section I serves as an introduction to the two major Fascists in *The Underground Stream*, Jeffrey Grebb, who is personnel director of Jefferson Motors in Detroit, and Harvey Kellog, the leader of the Detroit chapter of the Black Legion. Both men are first seen at the annual ball of the Kingston Country Club, and their behavior at the ball becomes a statement of their personalities. Grebb, like many self-made men, "despised upper class social life but yearned for the right to partake of it none the less." He wants to be made a member of the club not because he has an intrinsic interest in the club or its activities but because he wants the distinction of being a member. A large man who projects a sense of tremendous force, Grebb is the son of a packinghouse butcher in a Chicago slum and it gives him enormous delight to "bring his stockyard stink into a bailiwick of the old, envied class." He cares for nothing but power.

Harvey Kellog also wants power, although he is less obsessive (if more neurotic) than Grebb. Older than the personnel director of Jefferson Motors, Kellog is a striking-looking man, "bald, cadaverous of face almost to being ugly, with hollow-set, tortured eyes." He had gone bankrupt during the Depression, and his wife had died in childbirth. His daughter, Adelaide, has gradually become his one love, just as Roosevelt has become the symbol of all he despises. And as Jeffrey Grebb's one real passion is the possession of power for the sake of power, so Harvey Kellog's one passion is the Black Legion: Roosevelt was cutting the foundation of America from under the feet of all decent people, Kellog was convinced, and as a result, the "violence and plotting [of America's 'internal enemies'] must be met with greater violence."

Despite their Fascist temperaments and alliance with Fascist organizations, Grebb and Kellog have a basic dislike for each other. They have nothing in common but their Fascism. Kellog is a weak, frustrated insurance broker, a man who finds it impossible to sleep and can release his fears and anxieties only in the rituals and violence of the Black Legion; Grebb is strong-willed, intelligent, and ruthless, a man who believes that other men are valuable only to the extent that they give him power and women to the extent that they give him sexual pleasure. It is, in fact, in their attitude toward women and sex that the difference between the two men is most clearly delineated.

Kellog has never recovered from the shock of his wife's sudden death. After twenty-three years he still cries in bed at night and wonders if it is possible to love a dead woman for so long. Kellog's soul "was complexly wounded on the subject of women." Grebb, on the other hand, shares none of Kellog's hesitancies toward women: "Do you know the middle-class woman?" he asks at one point. "Useless as hell, most of them, but they're ripe plums. You don't know what a woman is if you never had one of that breed between the sheets." Grebb has "one of that breed" as his mistress, and it is with her that Section I of *The Underground Stream* ends.

As soon as he returns home from the country club ball, Grebb rings for his housekeeper-mistress, Shirley Thomas, a woman of twenty-six, who came to work for Grebb after her husband had been blinded in an accident in the Jefferson Motors factory. Their lovemaking, as always, satisfies Grebb for only a few minutes; then, as always, he drifts into fantasy, struggling against the horror of dying. And then the fantasy passes, and a surge of life returns: "Men lived and worked and died in blindness," Grebb ruminates, "but he would not. He would *use* life, he need not be used by it ... a man who was aware, who moved with the proper stream, could keep stepping up and up until the last moment of his existence. For such a man there was no limit to the power that could be achieved. He could hold all of life itself, its goods and chattels, in the cup of his hand...."

From Jeffrey Grebb and Shirley Thomas, Maltz shifts the scene to Fred Prince — known as Princey — and his wife, Betsy. Betsy is a year older than Shirley Thomas, and is as devoted to her husband as Shirley is to her lover. But Betsy is also devoted to the Communist Party (as is Princey), while Shirley Thomas is devoted only to Grebb and the comfort he can give her. To be with Grebb, Shirley agrees to leave her children; Betsy wants nothing more than to have a child — "I *need* a baby, Princey. I want one so much ... I'm twenty-seven already" — but a union organizer like Princey is always in danger of losing his job, so Betsy decides to wait: "If one of the sacrifices we have to make is not to have any children," she tells her husband, "then maybe that's how it'll have to be. We talk easily about revolutionaries having to make sacrifices — maybe this is what it means. It's come home now!"

The poignancy of Betsy's decision is in sharp contrast to that of Shirley Thomas, who, because she "loved the pretty things Grebb gave her" and "delighted in the good bed she slept in, the fine, new food, the household entrusted to her care," told herself each time she kissed her children good-bye that "it was best for them too." Equally stark in its contrast is the relationship between the two couples. Like a Pavlovian dog, Shirley appears whenever Grebb rings for her. But there is nothing so easy or crass in the life of Betsy and Fred Prince. Because she works in a laundry during the day and Princey has the night shift in the tool and die shop at Jefferson Motors, Betsy and Princey meet only on Sunday, and then only for that brief period between his awakening and the time she has to go to sleep. As a result, Betsy has become jittery; "as with a bride or a newly awakened girl, she was dominated by the superficial fevers of love, by unreal fantasies and hours of anxiety." She becomes angry when she learns that Princey has accepted a Party assignment on their one day together. Yet she understands the need for Princey to organize the unions, and she becomes equally enraged when he facetiously offers to quit the Party. (A member of the Young Communist League at seventeen, she reminds Princey that she "was an old war horse" while he was still playing soccer for the company union.)

Although Princey is the central character of *The Underground Stream* (or, better, the hero of the novel, for as Harold Strauss rightly observed in his review in the *New York Times,* Princey is indeed a hero for Maltz, not just a central character)[6], it is Betsy who dominates this particular section. And, again, this is in sharp contrast to the scene between Shirley and Grebb. In their bedroom scene, the conversation is really a monologue. Like Ferral in André Malraux's *Man's Fate* (whom he resembles in many ways)[7], Grebb flaunts his male ego, and Shirley makes the required, albeit sincere, responses:

"You belong to me, don't you?" he demanded.
"Yes, Jeffrey."
"You don't care for conventions, you just want to be loved, don't you?"
"Yes," she whispered.
Grebb stood up and took a step toward her. "You've got a lovely body, a good woman's body. Your body doesn't care about conventions, does it?"
Shirley trembled. She raised one hand to her breast. He came close to her. "You're mine, aren't you?"
"Yes."
"I can do what I want with you?"
"Yes, anything!"

He caught her arms, hurting the flesh. "And you love me, don't you?"
"Yes," she said, with a burst of passion, "oh, yes, yes!"

In the parallel scene with Betsy and Fred Prince, there is no
flaunting of egos, no quiescent surrender of one's dignity. They are
"comrades and lovers," husband and wife. They are, to be sure, as
concerned with the Party as Grebb is with personal power, but they
are also concerned for each other. "You know what our party is,
Princey?" Betsy asks her husband. "It's a cannibal. It eats up a
sincere comrade like you. And it has to be... It can't be concerned
with the personal problems of people like us. But it's up to each
individual to know how much he can do and how much he can't.
The Party takes that for granted." Princey knows how much he can
do. In a mock-serious voice he advises Betsy that "Man does not
live by politics alone," then embraces his wife, and the frustration
each feels at the need to be apart so often is forgotten in an afternoon of lovemaking. When Princey finally leaves for a Party meeting, Betsy's mind begins to wander; and, again, her fantasy is
singularly and emblematically different from Grebb's dream of
holding all of life in the cup of his hand: "She [Betsy] lay, a hand
on each breast, as though in demonstration of the overflowing con-
tentment in her heart. She listened to the ticking of the clock, wish-
ing she had some good, rich chocolate to eat. Some day she would
buy a box of candy, go home, lock the door, pull down the shades,
and gobble it all up herself."

At almost the exact time that Fred and Betsy Prince are demon-
strating the truth of Princey's dictum that "man does not live by
politics alone," the Black Legion is preparing to meet. After asking
his daughter to leave the house for a few hours — "Pussy, I'm
sorry to be so secretive about what I'm doing. Believe me, I do wish
I could tell you, because I know you'd be proud of me. Someday
you will know.... The whole country will know." — Harvey
Kellog goes into the basement of his home to await the arrival of
the new initiate, Jeffrey Grebb. The meeting, as Grebb observes,
has all the characteristics of a melodrama: an anonymous special
delivery letter telling him of the meeting, a rendezvous with an
unidentified person who escorts him to the secret meeting place, a
walk down unlit cellar steps, the necessary two knocks on the door,
and the inevitable password, "Place none but Americans on
guard." Despite the melodrama, however, Grebb finds something
terrifying about the whole sequence of events. As he enters the

basement room he tenses in an automatic reaction to what he sees:

Seated in the arc of the light were row upon row of masked figures. There seemed to be thirty or forty of them, each one bulking hugely, arms folded, torso rigidly erect. Their dress was black. On each head mask was a large, white skull above two crossed bones; on each dark chest, marking the heart, the same death's head lay glistening. It was the Ku Klux costume, he [Grebb] knew, but founded on black instead of white. And the effect was terrifying.

Two robed figures lead Grebb into the center of the room, and the voice of Harvey Kellog then asks, "Jeffrey Grebb, are you ready to undergo the formal initiation of the Bullet Clubs?" Grebb is quite ready and is told to get down on his knee; a loaded pistol is held to his heart and Kellog's solemn voice begins to read the oath:

In the name of God and the devil, one to reward, the other to punish, and by the powers of light and darkness, good and evil, here — under the black arch of heaven's avenging symbol — I PLEDGE AND CONSECRATE my heart, my body and my limbs, and swear, by all the powers of heaven and hell, to devote my life to the obedience of my superiors, and no danger or peril shall deter me from executing their orders.

I will exert every possible means in my power for the extermination of the anarchists, Communists, the Roman Hierarchy and their abettors.

Before violating a single clause or implied pledge of this, my obligation, I will pray to an avenging God and to an unmerciful devil to tear my heart out and roast it over flames of sulphur; that my head be split open, and my brains scattered over the earth, that my body be ripped up, my bowels be torn out and fed to the carrion birds, and that this punishment may be meted out to me through all eternity in the name of God our creator.

Grebb pledges to obey all the Legion asks of him and is allowed to stand. Kellog then resumes reading the articles of faith:

Jeffrey Grebb, you have signified your willingness to join our organization. We inform you that it is an organization of chivalry and daring. It follows in the footsteps of the guerrilla bands of the South which were famed during the Civil War for their courage and bravery, and which were marked as outlaws by their enemies. Now, you, like us, are outlawed indeed. We inform you that the Black Legion is obligated to the preservation of the white race. If America is a melting pot, the white people are neither the aristocratic scum on top nor the dregs of society on the bottom.

We regard as enemies of ourselves and our country all Aliens, Negroes, Jews and cults and creeds believing in racial equality and owing allegiance to any foreign potentate. We fight as guerrillas, using any weapon that comes to our hand. Mercy belongs only to sycophants; it emasculates soldiers.

A series of questions follows — "Do you believe in white supremacy, and that no Negro should have authority over a white man?" "Will you do all in your power to place only white Protestant Americans in public office?" — and, finally, as a token of membership, Grebb is given a thirty-eight caliber bullet.

Unlike Kellog, whose allegiance to the Black Legion is founded on "the passionate belief that the Legion would regenerate America," Grebb's motive for joining is devoid of any such commitment. His interest in the Legion is twofold. First, he sees the Legion as a possible force in combating the newly formed CIO. (One of his jobs at Jefferson Motors is to keep its plants non-union.) And, even more important perhaps, is his belief that sooner or later America would swing into Fascism, and "with the consciousness of the role that industry and capital must play in any Fascist movement, he saw no reason not to embark upon a political career." To this end he has made connections with several organizations and has very deliberately decided to join the Black Legion. When called upon to speak, Grebb thus begins to prepare the Legion to work for him:

I don't mind telling you [he says to the hooded figures] that we're expecting a little trouble [at Jefferson Motors] from this Red C.I.O. that's just been formed. We know that they got their plans all set to move in on Auto and carry on this organizing in Detroit. So all I want to say to you is this. If trouble does start in, if some of those paid agitators do succeed in turning the heads of some of our foreigners and Hunkies and general dumbheads — because remember they got an awful lot of Moscow money behind them trying to start a revolution — why, then that'll be our chance to replace every Catholic and nigger and alien in the plant by a real, honest-to-goodness, white, Protestant American. That's all I got to say to you now, Brothers."

A few minutes later, with Kellog urging the Black Legion to stop the American curse of too much liberty for anarchists, aliens, and agents of Moscow, the men of the Iron Guard begin to unmask and the meeting officially comes to an end.

The next section of *The Underground Stream* shifts back to Princey and the Communist sensibility. Unlike many intellectuals — no doubt like Maltz himself — who "ally themselves to the revolutionary moments of their time out of a vision of a new society, or from indignation at injustice, or from embittered idealism," Prince has become a Communist because of "daily events, his work and life — and among those events a tire chain wielded by a policeman." He accepts the responsibilities to which he has committed himself, and takes pride in the movement. Yet there are times when he wants an easier existence, when the demands of the Party seem too much: so, at least, Princey thinks to himself as he waits to meet Paul Turner, one of the Party leaders.

This scene parallels that in the preceding section in which Jeffrey Grebb is met in his car by a member of the Legion, is escorted to Kellog's cellar, and, after the initiation rites, listens to a speech by the General Organizer of the Black Legion, E. B. Curry. Princey, in turn, is escorted to his meeting with Turner by Jesse Vandermill, a laborer in the heavy forge department at Jefferson Motors, whose Party assignment is to be Princey's bodyguard. The meeting between Turner and Princey takes place not in a cellar but in Jesse's run-down car; it is unsafe for Princey to go to the Party office or for Turner to be seen going into Princey's house. Turner, like Curry, has stopped in Detroit on his way to Toledo; and, like the organizer of the Black Legion, he is totally devoted to his cause. But with the exception of their fair hair, there is no similarity between the two men. Curry, a former Detroit policeman who has lost a leg as a result of an automobile accident, is described as being "solid as a tree trunk, thick-necked, with a deeply pitted face and eyes like black olives. His hair was pure white, but instead of softening his appearance it only seemed to accentuate his primordial physical power." Turner's main physical characteristic is his ashen pallor — the stigma of chronic lead poisoning. "I got painter's colic, don't you know that?" he asks Princey. "I haven't done any painting for fifteen years, but even now I still can't smoke or drink; I have to watch my diet like a society beauty."[8]

Turner, not Princey, is the true Party functionary. Ready to accept anything that comes along, he provides the Party with "an essential element, a functionary of rock-like solidity and loyalty, a wheelhorse able to carry on year in and year out, irrespective of success or failure." He is a person of unshakeable devotion; and, as such, he is not above reproaching any individual who betrays the Party's principles. Thus, when Princey complains that Jesse Vandermill drives him "cuckoo," Turner reminds him that a person cannot work with the masses unless he is willing to accept them the way they are: "I'll tell you," says Turner, "impatience happens to be a weakness of yours, Princey. You ought to watch it. An attitude like this can lead to snobbery, it can lead to contempt for the masses. I'm serious about this. After all, who are we to look down our noses at Jesse? ... We're a political party trying to lead the working class, not social workers trying to uplift them three times a week."

Despite the harsh words, the two men are very fond of each other. Turner, in fact, has come to Detroit expressly to offer Princey a position in the Party's newly established National Training School; to Turner, "there's been no development in Party life more important than this." Princey is flattered, but he is torn by conflicting desires. The chance for solid study is attractive. But he would have to go without Betsy, and he knows that the Party would look upon his six months of education as an investment: he would no doubt be asked to become a full-time functionary. And Princey does not have Turner's dedication. The idea of becoming a Party functionary repels him: "It took a type of stamina, of dogged devotion, of moral inexhaustibility which he was not sure he had." So after only a few minutes of deliberation Princey decides against accepting the offer; and Turner, deeply disappointed, consoles himself with the old truth that "weak men make weak Communists, vain men make unreliable Communists — and a Party was made up of very human people indeed."

After Princey rejects Turner's offer the two men sit in uncomfortable silence until Princey announces that he no longer wants a bodyguard: "Roosevelt needs a bodyguard, not me," he snaps. "I'm a Liberty Leaguer." Turner tries to dissuade him by reminding him of the murder of Marchuck and of the vigilantism that has accompanied every attempt to unionize the auto industry. But Princey isn't convinced; and later that evening, after Jesse has driven him to the Party meeting, Princey insists that he not wait for him. Jesse protests but finally leaves, and for the first time in two months Fred Prince is without a bodyguard.

Two short sections conclude the first part of *The Underground Stream,* and, following the same pattern established earlier, the first of these sections moves back to Grebb and Kellog. The two men have returned to the latter's living room after the Legion meeting, and they very quickly get into a heated argument. Grebb disapproves of the vigilante techniques of the Legion, and he denounces the Iron Guard as being "nothing more than a hatchet gang." Kellog's angry rejoinder is that "The Iron Guard is a political weapon in the struggle against our enemies. In this world no one gets anywhere by talk. To compare our activities with gangsterism is nonsense." Grebb tries to convince Kellog that the Legion's methods are not realistic: "... You people seem to regard terror as an end. It's not an end; it never is! It's merely a useful weapon to be used discreetly. Yet you regard it as your main activity and that's what I'm kicking about. To become a political party capable of taking power we need mass agitation openly conducted. We will have our secret combat groups, of course. But from all I can see you people are limiting your activity to the equivalent of back-lot gang fights...." To which Kellog contemptuously responds, "Another theorist! Agitation by words! Pretty speeches! We seem to get one like you every six months." The argument is suddenly interrupted by the unexpected intrusion of Frank Speaight, Grebb's right-hand man, who informs his boss that Princey can be picked up "the way you want." The way Grebb wants Princey is without anyone knowing he is gone; otherwise he is of no use to him.

And that is exactly how Grebb gets him. As Princey is being driven home from the meeting, the car is stopped by Speaight and another man who pretend they are policemen and that the car Princey is riding in has been stolen. The driver of the car is a Black worker, Ambrose Bishop, who has recently joined the Party but who in fact is an informer for Grebb. Princey is forced into the "police" car, which quickly drives off. At first, Princey suspects nothing; then, he finds that he cannot think, "his mind seemed bursting with knowledge, but he could fasten on nothing coherent; it was as though his body and brain had dissolved into a cauldron of pure sensation." And then, abruptly, with an incommunicable sense of horror, he realizes that he is being kidnapped. But, just as abruptly, Speaight senses Princey's sudden awareness of the situation, and before he can do anything Princey is knocked unconscious.

With the kidnapping of Princey, the pace of *The Underground Stream* quickens. Maltz has lingered over the events leading to the abduction (Part I comprises almost half of the entire work), carefully delineating on alternate planes the Fascist and Communist sensibilities. But with the successful kidnapping of Princey, the contrapuntal structure is no longer employed; the two sensibilities now meet head on in the confrontation between Grebb and Princey.

Grebb has made Princey his prisoner, but he neither wants information from him nor does he wish to destroy him. He wants Princey to renounce the Party and join forces with him: nothing less will satisfy him. Grebb has read widely in Marxist literature,[9] and in an attempt to gull Princey he tells his captive that although he believes that "the Marxist analysis of capitalism is correct," he also believes that in a test of power between the forces of capitalism and Communism the progressive forces will be smashed by some form of Fascism. And the only way to prevent that, Grebb argues, is to overthrow Fascism — and that can only be done by working from within. "Men like you and me have one of two choices," Grebb tries to convince Princey. "We can work with the proletarian movement and be smashed; or we can choose a brilliant new political path." That path, of course, is the one Grebb has chosen: "To remain within the ranks of capital. To gain power in the growing Fascist movement! *And then to use that power to break up Fascism from within* — to bring Socialism quickly!"

When Princey scornfully refuses his "new political path," Grebb offers him a position of power, and when that is refused he tries to buy his support. But Princey remains adamant: "I'm afraid my ambitions ... don't take me so far," is his only reply to Grebb's offer. Grebb grows impatient and puts the point of a knife blade under Princey's fingernail. When he winces in pain, Grebb taunts him, then tells him that he doesn't want him that way: "I know you've got courage. You'd hold out until you were broken, but when you were broken you wouldn't be any more use to me. I can't have a broken man for this job." Before Princey can say anything, Grebb is informed that Betsy and several Party members, who have been feverishly searching for Princey, have discovered that Bishop was the informer and have gone to the police with trade union backing. That drastically changes the situation for both men. "From now on," a disturbed Grebb informs Princey, "you're very dangerous, unless you're with me. You're either with me now — or a real menace ... You either go out of here working for me, Princey, or not at all."

At this point, what Maltz referred to as the moral quest which gives *The Underground Stream* its "motor power" begins to dominate the novel. The struggle between the Fascist and Communist sensibilities becomes secondary to Princey's personal struggle against the imminence of his own death. Like the men in "Season of Celebration" who watch Jimmy O'Shaughnessy die, Princey suddenly becomes aware of a "foreign, tumeric body inside, attached there like a sponge, contracting and expanding with each movement of his lungs. Yet he knew what it was: pure phantom: the image of his fear, the choice he could not make." He had chosen to be a Communist because he had to be one, but he did not have to die now. And what was important was not only how you lived but how you died.

Princey dies with dignity. Fearful and lonely, he gains enormous strength from his hatred for Grebb. "I'm nothing," Princey tells his captor in a low-keyed voice, "but I'm tied to something big. I want to hold onto that. The thing I'm part of is living and what you're part of is stinking up the whole earth." Grebb, now openly contemptuous of Princey, offers him yet another chance to save his life. Princey says nothing. But to himself he thinks, *"Beneath all else is this: A man must hold to his purpose. This — nothing less — is the underground stream of his life. Without it he is nothing. I cannot yield! A man is nothing who yields his purpose."* Minutes later Harvey Kellog and the men of the Black Legion burst through the door and drag Princey to a waiting car. In the morning, a farm boy stumbles over Princey's body in a clump of woods: "Face up in the clear, cold sky, the body lay at full length, in singular repose. There was no agony in the final posture and no hurt. The bruised face was calm."

V   *A Left-wing Writer with Talent*

As was usual with Maltz's work, the reviews of *The Underground Stream* were mixed. In almost every instance, however, the character of Fred Prince was the focal point of the review. Lewis Gannett, for example, who no doubt had the last scene of the novel in mind, wrote that with a few changes *The Underground Stream* might well have been about an early Christian martyr.[10] Mike Gold, in his review for the *Daily Worker,* took a more partisan attitude. He saw Fred Prince not as a Christian martyr but as a man symbolic of the "Promethean courage" of ordinary baseball-loving Americans; and, as such, he concluded that the ending of *The Underground Stream* was not true and complete. "After all," Gold wrote, "an industrial auto union was formed, and despite the Grebbs, it did grow into a national power. It was the workers who won, and not their capitalistic torturers."[11]

Not all the reviewers, of course, regarded Princey as either a modern-day Christ or a Prometheus. To Louis Filler and Ralph Thompson, Princey was simply a Communist, Maltz a Communist sympathizer, and, consequently, *The Underground Stream* was a complete failure. "To believe in the book at all," Thompson wrote in the *New York Times,* "one has to be ready to agree that Princey ... has died for a noble and sacred ideal. I am sorry, but I can't begin to agree." Almost as an afterthought, Thompson added: "I wonder whether Princey would agree had he lived until 1939 or 1940."[12] The same political judgment was made by Louis Filler, who commented that the readers of the novel were not likely to be charmed into forgetting such recent events as the Nazi-Soviet pact; although Maltz seems to believe that the struggle for social justice must proceed underground, Filler wrote, " 'the Left' is shame-faced and apologetic today and even 'the party' swears formal loyalty to the Constitution."[13] Fortunately, this kind of irrelevant criticism did not dominate the reviews. Such influential critics as Harry Hansen and Alfred Kazin were more sympathetic to Maltz's art as well as his politics; and, even more important, they were able to distinguish between the two. Thus, to Hansen, Princey is indeed a martyr, but "when he takes it on the chin we think of him not as a radical standing up for his convictions but as a human being abused by thugs."[14] And Kazin, who regarded Maltz as a "Left-Wing writer with real talent," concluded his very favorable review of the novel by noting that although important qualities were lacking in *The Underground Stream,* "there are other virtues in the novel, other ambitions, greater excellences; these may be enough at the moment, these are warm and arresting now."[15]

VI   The Reality of Death

Two stories remain to be considered here, "Sunday Morning on Twentieth Street" and "Afternoon in a Jungle."[16] They make an apt conclusion to this chapter for, though slight stories, they are concerned with Maltz's two major themes: the failure of the American system and what Chester Eisinger has called "the psychic reality of death."[17]

Death is ever-present in Maltz's work: in *Merry Go Round,* in *Peace on Earth,* in *The Way Things Are,* and, as we shall see, it is in his later works as well. At times, Maltz's concern with death is primarily for the dramatic effect it creates: the executions of Ed Martin (*Merry Go Round*) and Peter Owens (*Peace on Earth*), for example, serve as the ultimate castigation of a corrupt society. But more often — and this in part is why his work is superior to that of most left-wing writers — death rather than hunger and strikes dominated Maltz's imagination. Jimmy O'Shaughnessy dies "from not having a job," but the story's power is in the reaction of the men in the flophouse to his death; it is *their* fear of death, *their* awareness that there is something more horrifying than the awfulness of their own existence that makes the story so effective. It is not the silicosis of Jack Pickett that makes "Man on the Road" memorable but the way he faces his death. And it is not so much the economic plight of Jesse — the happiest man on earth — that finally absorbs the reader's attention as it is his preference for and joy in the face of death. So, too, it is death that dominates the whole of "Sunday Morning on Twentieth Street."

Like "Season of Celebration," "Sunday Morning on Twentieth Street" is a mood story rather than a story of action. A young girl has committed suicide, and the people on Twentieth Street wait for her body to be taken away. But here death is not the transfiguring experience it was in "Season of Celebration." In the Hotel Raleigh each man instinctively responds to O'Shaughnessy's pain and eventual death; devoid of any sense of security, O'Shaughnessy's agony becomes a touchstone of their own fear. But on Twentieth Street most of the onlookers are young boys to whom death is a physical rather than a psychic reality. Death has become an all-too-common occurrence on their street; they have grown accustomed to the sound of sirens and the sight of a suicide being taken to the morgue. (Last week it was an old man, now it is a young girl.) To the younger children it is all fascinating and incomprehensible, while to the older boys the removal of the girl's body demands a moment of intense silence. And to the few adults on the street the new suicide once again raises the question of whether "Them that kills themselves is crazy" or whether "They ain't crazy . . . they's sorrowful." The question, however, is not debated. For whether they are sorrowful or crazy, the fact is, as one boy murmurs, "That's the way it is. I'm used to it." So is everyone else on Twentieth Street: the landlady wastes no time in hanging a "Vacancy" sign, one child begins to sing "Oh, ashes to ashes . . . Oh, ashes to ashes," and before long the streets are once again filled with boys playing ball.

The implied cause for the suicides in "Sunday Afternoon on Twentieth Street" is the failure of the capitalistic system. In "Afternoon in a Jungle" this failure is explicitly stated. The second of Maltz's stories to be published in *The New Yorker,* it might well have carried the title of the earlier work, "Incident on a Street Corner." For "Afternoon in a Jungle" *is* about an incident on a street corner, an incident in which a thirteen-year-old boy — who dreams of kissing Anita Louise and who receives a penny a week for candy — struggles with a small, shabby man of forty-five for a fifty-cent piece which has fallen through a subway grille.

And just as the boys in "Sunday Afternoon on Twentieth Street" cannot feel the meaning of death the way the men do in "Season of Celebration" — indeed, just as the policemen in "Incident on a Street Corner" cannot understand the hostility of the crowd — so the boy in the "jungle" cannot understand the desperation of the man who tries to fish up the coin from the subway pit. The boy has his dreams and fantasies, and the fifty cents will enable him to buy all the candy he wants. The man, one of America's bottom dogs, has nothing. He wants to share the money with young Charles Fallon, but the boy adamantly insists that he wants it all. "Jesus Christ! I got to have some of it," the grayish-faced man cries. "This is my *business,* kid. It's all I do. Can't you understand? I've been walking all day, I ain't found a thing. You got to let me have some of it. You got to!" But Charles won't share his find, and he won't listen to the shame-filled voice which asks, "Do you think I like to do this? If you was ten years older I could talk to you. You'd understand." Enraged, the boy snaps, "If I was ten years older I'd beat your face in."

Defeated by a boy too filled with his own fantasies and greed to understand the needs of another, the old man walks slowly away, leaving Charles standing on the corner triumphant and stonefaced. The victory is an empty one, however; it has become dark and it will be impossible for Charles to locate the coin. It is an ironic ending whose poignancy is intensified by its foreshadowing of Maltz's own future. For by the end of the 1940s, Maltz was to find himself not poverty-stricken like the man in "Afternoon in a Jungle" but an outcast nevertheless. America was about to begin its purge of the Left, and Maltz was shortly to be imprisoned (after which he would go into self-exile in Mexico). It was to be a dark time indeed for the dreamers of a new world.

CHAPTER 6

The Hollywood Years

I N June, 1941, just five months after the publication of "Afternoon in a Jungle," Maltz left New York for Hollywood. He had been teaching playwriting at New York University where he was paid according to the number of students who attended the course. The impending entry of the United States into the war resulted in a drastic reduction in enrollment, and Maltz decided to follow his friends George Sklar and Michael Blankfort to Hollywood. He was to remain there for nine years, during which time he wrote the scripts for such outstanding films as *This Gun for Hire* (1942), *Destination Tokyo* (1944), *Pride of the Marines* (1945), *The House I Live In* (1945), *Cloak and Dagger* (1946), and *The Naked City* (1948).

Maltz abandoned his brief academic career in the same year in which John Crowe Ransom published his literary manifesto, *The New Criticism*. There is, of course, no real connection between the two events; yet, the coincidence is striking. For although the literature of the 1930s was clearly dominated by left-wing writing, the upsurge in "proletarian" literature was paralleled from the very beginning of the decade by a resurgence of Humanistic writing. And just as Mike Gold's attack on Thornton Wilder in 1930 marked the emergence of a powerful radical voice whose concerns would be the focus of attention for most the decade, so the publication in 1930 of the Agrarian manifesto, *I'll Take My Stand,* offered a statement of conservatism that was to be a viable alternative to the literary and social revolutions of the 1930s. Indeed, *I'll Take My Stand* may well have attracted considerably less attention upon its publication than did Gold's "Wilder: Prophet of the Genteel Christ," but its impact has been far greater.

The literary doctrines of the Agrarians — now known as the New Critics — became the crux of Robert Penn Warren and Cleanth Brooks' extremely popular textbook, *Understanding Poetry* (1939). The success of this volume, and of Ransom's *The New Criticism,* foreshadowed the tie between academic theory and literary productivity, which was to become a salient feature of the literature of the 1940s. It also served to mark the failure of the literary Left in America: just as the thirties began with the Depression and its literary concomitant, proletarian literature, so it ended with the start of World War II and *its* literary concomitant, the New Criticism.

As such left-wing stalwarts as Maltz, Sklar, Blankfort and Trumbo were making their way to Hollywood, the New Criticism became a way of life in the academic world: the literary radicals were replaced by the returning soldiers who, with the G. I. Bill at their disposal, began once again to fill the universities. Under the aegis of the New Criticism, the social concerns of the thirties were replaced by an interest in the individual psyche; and, once again, American literature, as written and taught, turned inward. The writers on the Left soon became pariahs, subjects for the blacklist, Joe McCarthy, and out-of-print bookshops; the New Critics, on the other hand, became the subject of intensive classroom discussion, *PMLA,* and hundreds of university-sponsored little magazines.

I   *The War Novel*

The year after he arrived in Hollywood, Maltz began work on a new novel. The events of the time were of course providing writers with an obviously dramatic subject. *For Whom the Bell Tolls,* Ernest Hemingway's Spanish Civil War novel — the best of a long list on the subject — was published in 1940, and, with only a few exceptions, was the last work of fiction on that war for more than a decade. In the forties and fifties writers naturally enough turned their attention to *the* war, World War II.[1] John Steinbeck's *The Moon Is Down* and William Woods's *The Edge of Darkness* both appeared in 1942, and both were concerned with the Nazi occupation of Norway. Two years later, with the publication of Harry Brown's *A Walk in the Sun* and John Hersey's *A Bell for Adano,* the locale shifted to Italy and the focus of attention became the American soldier. These novels, in turn, were followed by a spate of excellent stories which eventually covered virtually every area and aspect of the war. (The best of these works probably are Alfred Hayes's *All Thy Conquests* [1946], Robert Lowry's *Casualty* [1946], John Horne Burns's *The Gallery* [1947], Vance Bourjaily's *The End of My Life* [1947], Norman Mailer's *The Naked and the Dead* [1948], James Gould Cozzens's *Guard of Honor* [1948], Irwin Shaw's *The Young Lions* [1948], John Hawkes's *The Cannibal* [1949], Herman Wouk's *The Caine Mutiny* [1951], and James Jones's *From Here to Eternity* [1951].)

Maltz's war novel, *The Cross and the Arrow,* was published in 1944 and, as one might expect, differed considerably from most of the war stories of the period. There are no battles in *The Cross and the Arrow,* no Captain Queegs, Maggios, and Ackermans, no Americans. The novel, to be sure, is prefaced by a quotation from Whitman's *Leaves of Grass,* and it was Maltz's hope that *The Cross and the Arrow* would be applied to the racist history of the United States.[2] But the novel took its impetus from events in Germany and was concerned with the German mind.

II   *Vansittartism*

Maltz has related the background for the writing of *The Cross and the Arrow* as follows: "The beginning of my political life more or less coincided with the rise of fascism. Like many others of my generation, I paid the closest attention to events in Germany, read intensively on it, met and talked with German refugees, and became good friends with several. Since the existence of German fascism was a dynamically evil force in European events from 1933 on, this preoccupation on my part was a daily affair, not a sometime one."[3]

With the operation of the Nazi war machine in Poland, Holland, Greece, and Yugoslavia, and "the fact that the Hitler Establishment had mass support from a very large section of the German people, a debate arose in the U.S. and England about the German people as people."[4] In England, Baron Robert Gilbert Vansittart, a British diplomat, enunciated the doctrine (which was to take the name of Vansittartism) that served as the focal point for much of the debate. According to Vansittart, the German people as a race were addicted to war; from the time of the Franco-Prussian war, he contended, they had supported, and continued to support, the militaristic and aggressive policies of their leaders. It was essential, therefore, that the German people be forced to undergo a corrective program which would educate them to be a less military people. Should this program fail, it would then be necessary to exterminate them.

What particularly disturbed Maltz about Vansittartism was that it "began to find increasing support, even amongst people who presumably should have known better: some Marxists, for instance." (Ilya Ehrenbourg is cited by Maltz as an example of a Marxist "who seemed to have lost all perspective" about the German people when he accompanied the Russian troops who were retaking territory after the Nazis were defeated on Moscow fronts in late 1941.) Maltz's own attitude was unwavering:

As a matter of principle [he wrote in 1969] I could not accept a racist judgement about any people. Furthermore, I could not politically lump the three wars Vansittart used [the War of 1872, World Wars I and II] as evidence in one box. Each war in my opinion had a different origin, and no one of them was due to a war-like virus in the German bloodstream. Nevertheless, an explanation was needed of the way in which the German people, in such large proportion, seemed to be: (1) supporting the Hitler regime (2) willingly enjoying the loot sent back to them by their sons from Holland, Norway, France, etc. (3) willingly fighting and dying to conquer other peoples.[5]

His answer to this moral-political problem was *The Cross and the Arrow*.

III   The Cross and the Arrow

Since *The Cross and the Arrow* was written at least in part as a rejoinder to the doctrine of Vansittartism, it is not surprising that the thesis of the novel is a denial of Vansittart's racist theory. The human being, Maltz argues, "is born neither good nor evil, but can, by circumstances or pressures, be led in varied directions."[6] It is this belief that controls the movement and structure of *The Cross and the Arrow*.

What strikes one's attention most immediately about Maltz's second novel is that the dramatic climax occurs before the novel begins: as we learn at the outset, Willi Wegler, the hero of *The Cross and the Arrow*, is dying in a Nazi hospital, having been shot in the abdomen by a member of the S.S. who saw Willi trying to signal the British RAF. There is no chance that he will survive the wound. As such, the dramatic impetus of the novel comes not from learning *what* finally happens but *why* it happens. This not only enables Maltz once again to focus upon the way a man faces his death, it allows him to center all his attention upon the issues raised by the doctrine of Vansittartism, which Maltz does by responding to the question asked by an S.S. interrogator: "Who is Wegler, what is he?" — this trusted German factory worker who had just been awarded the War Labor Medal and who suddenly and seemingly inexplicably has betrayed the Nazis by shooting a flaming arrow of hay into the sky at the exact moment that British planes were flying over the camouflaged tank factory.

Who was Willi Wegler? His dossier answers that question: a German born of German parents; his wife killed in a British bombing raid; his son, a lance corporal in the Waffen S.S., killed at Narvik and posthumously awarded the Iron Cross; a Lutheran who did not attend church; inactive in politics both before and after the Third Reich. Thus, like W. H. Auden's "Unknown Citizen," the State can proclaim of Willi Wegler: "May be considered definitely friendly. Cell leaders regard him as a solid, patriotic German." This much the records make clear. But they offer no clues — indeed, they only make more complex the question of what sort of man "this exemplary German worker" is: an agent of British intelligence? Or one of the "Red scum in the factory? *What?*"

The answer to the *what* — to why Willi Wegler wanted to direct the British planes to the factory where he had worked industriously as a drop-forge man — is the subject of "The Investigation," the first and major part of the novel. Employing a structure similar to that of *The Underground Stream,*[7] *The Cross and the Arrow* encompasses only twelve hours of an August day in 1942, with "The Investigation" taking place from 11 P.M. until 6 A.M. And during this time, as a half-conscious Willi Wegler reflects in silence upon the events which led to his firing the flaming arrow, a host of characters, including Berthe Linng, Willi's mistress and fiancée, Julius Baumer, Labor Front leader of the factory, Adolf Kehr, Gestapo commissar, and Dr. Herman Zoder, the factory physician — seek to resolve the paradox of Willi Wegler.

But the paradox for these people remains unresolved, as it must; indeed, the motivating force of Willi's act of sabotage is defined by Maltz largely in terms of the very inability of the people who surround Willi to understand him. Baumer and Kehr, for example: each unimpressed with the other, yet both totally dedicated to the Third Reich.

Baumer is seen as the Nazi functionary, "a worn, driven man . . . with bitter lines cut fine around his mouth." In 1929, a university graduate with a degree in architecture, Baumer was a defeated man: no job, no money, no prospects, and no hope. Then, by chance, "he came upon his future" — a soup kitchen established by the National Socialist Party. There, in addition to a daily bowl of soup, he found the opportunity to earn some money by handing out leaflets, and he learned that there were rooming houses where young Nazis could sleep on the floor without cost. Within a week Baumer had joined the Party and his self-respect had returned. Yet it was the deepest irony of Baumer's life that the years that followed had been bitterly disappointing:

It was not his personal career that troubled him, but Germany. Month after month he had waited for the full Party program to materialize. . . . And as it did not, he had become more and more uneasy. He would lie awake at night and argue with himself: on the one hand Germany was rearming and becoming strong. He wanted that! The pledge to liquidate unemployment had been kept; the unity of the nation, the foreign policies, were being brilliantly achieved. But on the other hand — where was the Party promise to limit all salaries to one thousand marks a month? What about the liquidation of profiteering — or the protection of small business? For years he had given his heart's blood to a program that would be both National and Socialist. Why was it, he asked himself, that only half of that program was being carried out now? He found no answer, and each month brought a new question, a new bitterness. By the time the war came he was an unhappy and disillusioned man.

Even the position of Labor Front leader of a tank factory failed to reawaken Baumer's enthusiasm; the ecstasy was gone, "the dream was still unfulfilled. . . . The promise had been temporarily . . . postponed. . . ." Despite the disillusionment, however, Baumer is a Party fanatic, the sort, as Gestapo Commissar Kehr decides upon his first meeting with the Labor Front leader, "you can tell by his smell. One of those long-haired idealists who have to be buttered with slogans."

Kehr, for his part, is disdainful of fanatics like Baumer. A member of the Gestapo for only two months, Kehr is primarily a detective; and, unlike Baumer, his position is that of a government employee who had been granted special permission to join the Party after the National Socialists took power. This, of course, puts Kehr in an inferior category to Baumer but Kehr feels he can afford to be philosophical about his position:

The Baumers came and the Baumers went [Kehr tells himself] — but it was men like himself who survived in the long run. In thirty years of police work he had served under more chiefs than he could recall, and he had watched official heads roll under political winds while his own remained nicely cushioned on its sturdy neck, thank you. It made him laugh to think of it. The truth was that he — Adolf Kehr — *was* the State. The State wasn't the Kaiser — because the Kaiser was gone. Noske wasn't the State, nor was Ebert or Rathenau. Everybody knew their names and nobody had heard of Kehr. But where were they today? A simple question, yet when he put it that way, all things became clear. Yes. . . . He could afford to let a Party radical look down his nose at him. The radicals had their day, and then they invariably vanished. It was men like him who continued right on, providing the State with its backbone.

Kehr, then, like Baumer, belongs to the State; and like Baumer, he can neither understand nor tolerate the acts of any man that go contrary to the will of the State.

Herman Zoder and Berthe Lingg are more interesting because they are more complex than either Baumer or Kehr. The latter seldom become more than personifications of the State; Zoder and Berthe Lingg, on the other hand, while representative of those who are controlled by the State, are portrayed by Maltz not as stock figures but as individuals whose reactions to the force of the Nazi machine are marked by the complexity and anguish of human choice.

Zoder was appointed factory physician because he was a good doctor and a good German. Or so it seemed: for "Herman Zoder, the man, had nothing in common with what Baumer thought of him, or what a nurse thought of him. It was true of Zoder, as it is to a lesser degree of all men, that he led two lives — one with his fellow men and one eternally alone." The Zoder known to the Nazis and the workers in the factory was "a patriotic German, a self-sacrificing doctor, and a mirthful fool." Such was the appearance. The reality of Herman Zoder was that of a soul squeezed dry, "a heart no longer capable of emotion, a bitter bleakness in which love, pity, vanity were no more than pellets of dung from a life past and forgotten."

Zoder knew only one emotion, hatred — hatred for all that was German. In the latter half of the 1920s he had steadfastly refused to believe that intelligent people would take seriously the activities of Hitler and his followers. And later, when the Nazis grew powerful, Zoder insisted that even if Hitler did become chancellor, Germany would still continue on its democratic way: "No one could turn a society on its head," he argued. "That was unthinkable." It was after the Reichstag fire that Zoder's faith in his fellow Germans began to turn to contempt: "Like many another decent German, he became a cynical frightened human being who threw up his hands and kept quiet, and who became over the years increasingly regimented, increasingly terrified, increasingly cynical." Then the contempt turned into a violent, uncontrolled hatred. Ellie Beck, Zoder's daughter, was ordered to stand trial as being politically unfit to educate her child; and, rather than comply with the order, Ellie killed her child and herself. From that moment on Zoder's hatred became all-consuming and was projected in a terrifying dream: "There would be a plague. Within the space of a day, it would strike down every living German. And he, Zoder, would walk through the streets and cities and villages piled with corpses. He would do so because he had been assigned a task by God: to count every last corpse until it was certain that every last German had died. And then he, too, would die for he, too, was German."

Zoder's dream eventually becomes a "waking fantasy"; it is for this alone that he lives. And it is this creed that the wounded Willi Wegler threatens. As factory physician, Zoder must try to keep Willi alive, for Baumer and Kehr have many questions to ask him. But by shooting the flaming arrow Willi has separated himself from other Germans, and by so doing has indirectly challenged the principles of Zoder's very existence. For Zoder recognizes that Wegler cannot be hated as he hates other Germans. But, "his mind, keener than his heart, warned that if he helped a German, he would destroy the basis by which he lived." Thus, though Zoder, like Baumer and Kehr, asks *"Who was Wegler? what was he?"* the question for Zoder is really an attempt to define his own being and not that of the drop-forge worker; for Zoder, the actions of Willi Wegler serve essentially as the catalyst by which he is forced to reexamine his moral sensibility.

Unlike Herman Zoder, Berthe Lingg is exactly what she appears to be: a simple farm woman who is uninterested in politics but is a believer in the State. A "better" person than Kehr and Baumer, it is she who unwittingly compels Willi to his act of betrayal; and it is she who is the cause of Willi's being shot. Her story, and that of Willi Wegler, are inseparable, and what "The Investigation" fails to resolve about the paradox of Willi is resolved in "The Wrath of Jehovah," the second part of *The Cross and the Arrow.*

Berthe and Willi meet by accident and quickly become lovers: "Between them [Maltz writes] there was a ripening love of a man and woman, who were lonely and well-met; but beneath the adult love Willi was welded to this woman as a child to mother, seeing in her a radiance of adoration." And, indeed, they are well-met: simple, good people who want nothing more than to be together, to talk and to make love. But there is a profound difference in their simplicity, and, as a result, thoughts often remain unspoken. Of the two, only Willi has been at all disturbed by the events in Germany, only he had suddenly realized that "the world had spun one day when he was busy dreaming, and that it had whirled quite out of his reach." But even then Willi had no particular principle by which to combat the changes, no wish for anything but his work, his family, his cold water flat. He never understands about the Nazis; he only senses that a "rottenness" has come from them. And only slowly, and only because Berthe Lingg does not understand, does this vague sense turn to anger, and then to shame.

Berthe does not understand about her son, Rudi, for example. A member of the Nazi army, he has returned from France with a beautiful sweater for his mother. But the sweater, Rudi tells Willi, had been taken from a wealthy Frenchwoman whom the Nazis had raped and then arressted. Willi tries to make Berthe understand: "It's that Rudi wasn't *ashamed,*" he tells her. "Men do terrible things, I know. When you've been in a war and seen men die all around you, you change, I know that. Once I killed a Frenchman with a knife; I stabbed him in the throat. When men do things like that, a stay in trenches for months, it's not so hard for them to forget decency, to see a woman and to take her by force, perhaps. But after I killed that Frenchman, I wasn't happy... I've seen soldiers after they've handled a woman in the way Rudi and the others handled that Frenchwoman. There was always a — sickness in their faces. They wanted to forget what they did. They weren't proud of it, Berthe. Rudi was *proud.*"

Nor does Berthe understand about the Polish prisoners, four thousand of whom have been brought to the small village near Düsseldorf, most to be trained for jobs in the factory, a few to be used on the farms. Willi first hears about the prisoners at the factory, where the workers complain that they will have to train the Poles; they, after all, are Germans, not Polacks. Willi listens to the talk of his companions in uneasy silence. "Yes," he thinks, "this is how it is. This rottenness is here, too. A German, not a Polack. To a Polack or a Frenchwoman you can do what you want. There is no shame in what you do to them." As Willi continues to listen to his companions, a feeling of hatred begins to overwhelm him, "a violent, consuming hatred that blazed in his gut like a flame'; it was a hate as painful to Willi as was the throbbing in his stomach that came from the beat of the drop-forge at which he worked (and as that which would come from the bullet that would soon be throbbing deep in the core of his gut). The indecencies of Nazi Germany were becoming a monstrous obscenity, and with the arrival of the Polish prisoners Willi's soul began "groping towards an elemental gesture of protest."

Because Berthe does not understand, she buys a prisoner to work on her farm. All the farmers who can afford to, do so. "They're not cheap," she tells Willi, "seventeen marks I had to pay." When Willi reacts with disbelief that she would pay money for another person, Berthe admonishes her lover: "But how silly you are!" she roughly replies to Willi. "These are prisoners. I didn't buy a man in the way you mean it. I merely paid the government to have a man work on my farm while the war lasts. Everybody does that." Willi asks Berthe to return the prisoner but she is adamant: "I have to be practical," she cries furiously. "You and me alone — we can't save my hay now, or even harvest next month. So what should I do — lose my farm — starve — kill myself over a stinking Polack? So if the government rents me a Polish prisoner and says 'You'll pay *us* his wages, not him' — what am I to do? Did I make him a prisoner? Am I to blame that he went to war with us? No, I'm not to blame! All I know is that now I can ask for labor help — I won't lose my farm."

Willi does not respond. There isn't anything to say: Berthe, like Germany itself, has suddenly become a stranger. And so, like Abraham bearing Isaac in his arms to appease the wrath of Jehovah, Willi leaves the farmhouse and walks implacably, with a blind need, toward the barn, "carrying in his heart a burnt offering." Willi wants to help the prisoner escape and calls to the astonished figure cowering in the barn, "I'm a German, but I don't hate you. I wouldn't lock you up in a barn, or buy you for money like you were an animal. You're a man and I'm a man. I want to help you. Do you understand me, Bironski? I'm a German, but I want to help you. I have pity on you." From the darkness of the barn comes the forlorn, miserable plea of a man who cannot believe that any German would want to help a Pole: "Go away," he cries. "Don't make trouble for me. Please sir."

The next day Willi is awarded the Service Cross "as the exemplary type of worker in this great tank arsenal" by Julius Baumer. For most people it is a great if unexpected honor; for Willi it is an award that so fills him with shame that he can no longer deceive himself about his own complicity. The previous evening he had gone to Berthe Lingg's barn not so much to help the Polish prisoner as to relieve himself of a moral burden; had the Pole accepted his offer of help, it is possible that Willi would have found his absolution in that one act — and thereafter have shut his eyes to the outside world. But when he is rejected by Bironski, "it was as though a suffering Catholic child had been rejected by his priest."

So it is that at the moment that the Cross is pinned upon his breast, Willi finally understands that "he, too, was guilty, and no less guilty than all the rest ... that by his faithful work at the steam hammer, he, too, had enslaved these Poles ... that he, too, has carried a dead woman's sweater to Berthe Lingg, along with Rudi ... that he, too, had bought a Pole in the town square for seventeen marks — and that he had done these things by complicity, by his work and his silence — and that he, too, was stained by guilt." That night, Willi finally acts: he fashions new-cut hay in a field in the shape of an arrow, pointing in the direction of the factory, and as the British planes fly over the town he sets the hay on fire. As the arrow begins to blaze, the silence of the night is pierced first by Berthe's shrill screams of "They'll bomb us! They'll bomb us!", then by hoarse cries, and then by rifle shots. Not until 11 A.M. the following day, when the British planes return and begin to drop their bombs, does Willi know that his signal had been seen — "that this small deed he had done would weigh, and would be weighed."

Willi's awareness of his own complicity, and the actions he takes as a result of this awareness, are clearly Maltz's rejoinder to the racist doctrine of Baron Vansittart. But Maltz was not content to refute Vansittartism by the implications of Wegler's consciousness. It was imperative that he reject such a theory by direct statement, and he does just this through the character of Pastor Jakob Frisch, whose sensibility dominates "The Vision of Jakob Frisch," the third and final section of *The Cross and the Arrow*.

Baumer and Kehr never understand nor do they ever agree upon the cause of Willi's act of sabotage. To Kehr, temporary insanity is the only plausible explanation; to Baumer, the *quality* of Wegler's act makes it clear that the action was politically motivated. Both agree, however, that Bironski, the Polish prisoner, must be made the scapegoat (a decision that infuriates Berthe, who remarks bitterly, "and I'm to be without a Pole, I suppose? Seventeen marks I paid for him."). Of all the people who come in contact with Willi Wegler, only Jakob Frisch understands.

Years earlier, Jakob Frisch had been the pastor of a congregation which included Herman Zoder, and it was in front of this congregation that Frisch took his first stand against the Nazis. "As a citizen I will serve the State unto my death," Pastor Frisch told the congregation, which on this particular Sunday included a row of Storm Troopers. "But as a Christian I will resist the interference of the State with my Church unto the same death." That evening, with head shaved, eye-glasses smashed, and a sign reading I AM A SLAVE OF THE JEWS, Pastor Frisch was taken to a concentration camp. And now, after many years of bitterness, frustration, and disbelief, the act of Willi Wegler once again gives Jakob Frisch a sense of human dignity; he once again feels that he has "found the meaning of man's existence on this earth. And presently, presently, he knew he would find again the God he had also lost."

Because he believes in Willi, Frisch tries to convince the bewildered Doctor Zoder that all Germans are not alike; that he, Zoder, must choose between Wegler and Baumer. A "debate" takes place: Zoder becomes the spokesman for Vansittartism; Frisch becomes the voice of Albert Maltz. Zoder insists that he must have a constant principle if he is to live, and that for him the principle has become his distrust for all Germans — for Baumer, for the Pastor, for Wegler, even for himself. "All over Germany housewives feel the muscles of Polish girls, and men examine the teeth of Russian, Slovak and God knows what other miserable human beings, and then buy them as work slaves. Is it to be believed? Yes, it's happening. Human flesh is being sold in our streets," Zoder screams at Frisch. And then, in a whisper, "Damn them, damn them ... for now and unto eternity, damn them. This is a tainted people! This is the race dedicated to conquest. For seventy years we've been at it. All of us."

Frisch insists that a distinction must be made, that "Wegler is not Baumer. He is a German, yes, but no Baumer." Nor is the morality of the German soul such that it wants to conquer the world: "There is no fixed destiny to any people," Frisch tries to convince Zoder. "Do you think I condone crimes? There are Germans who are beyond redemption, yes! Who should know that better than I? Who broke my body but Germans? But I ask you: Are vile men new to this world? Have no other people seen it? And I ask you further: How has all of this come about? You're a scientist, you say. Will you show me this destiny in the German bloodstream? Is it some mystic infection?'' The problem for Zoder, Frisch argues, is not Wegler nor even Germany itself; rather, it is the spectacle of man, the inhumanity of the time, and the need to condemn blindly and totally. But, Frisch tells Zoder, in Willi Wegler's act of sabotage, in his need to refute the buying and selling of human beings, in his sense of guilt, was to be found the refutation of all racist theories as well as the indication of what man is, and what his morality is, and what man's future can be. For ''only in the wreckage of this madhouse,'' Frisch cries impassionedly, ''can something new be built.''

Slowly, almost reluctantly, Zoder understands what Frisch has been arguing, and instead of injecting Willi with strychnine as Baumer orders, he injects water. Willi is thus spared the torture awaiting him, and dies in peace as the British planes bomb the factory and Jakob Frisch writes on little sheets of paper, ''Willi Wegler — not Pole — lit fire to British. Proof — Wegler is in hospital — shot. Hitler leads us to disaster. Follow Wegler. Sabotage!''

IV   A New Stature

The Cross and the Arrow was the best received of all of Maltz's work. For once there was no disagreement between the *New York Times* and *New Masses;* both regarded the novel as a ''distinguished'' book which marked an important advance in Maltz's stature as a writer. Samuel Sillen, expressing the sentiments of the left-wing press, extolled *The Cross and the Arrow* as ''an intensely dramatic, thought-compelling novel,'' which represented a leap forward for Maltz as well as for American fiction of World War II. ''Able as his previous work had been,'' Sillen wrote in the *New Masses* of October 3, 1944, ''nothing that Albert Maltz has written approaches the new book in psychological depth, emotional force, artistic mastery.''[8] Orville Prescott, then the regular book reviewer for the *New York Times,* spoke about the novel in surprisingly similar terms: *The Cross and the Arrow,* Prescott wrote on September 22, 1944, ''is a sound, thoughtful and thoroughly interesting work. It is much the best thing Mr. Maltz has yet written and he has already written much. . . . With 'The Cross and the Arrow' he has achieved a new stature, for this is not a rigidly doctrinaire book. It is written with force and fury, but the breadth of its sympathies and the scope of its vision of humanity are not confined within a narrow pattern."[9] And just as Sillen had contended in the pages of *New Masses* that "Like every novel of stature, *The Cross and the Arrow* transcends its particular subject matter, enabling us to understand human types everywhere," so George F. Whicher wrote in the *New York Herald Tribune:* "Mr. Maltz has taken a theme of central importance to our time and treated it with a large-minded wisdom that can never go out of date. Few novels offer greater reward than this."[10]

Almost twenty years later, at least one critic would find that the "large-minded wisdom" had indeed gone out of date, that Maltz's Whitmanian optimism appeared "tenderminded and anachronistic in a world that has produced the existentialists, who see the shallow bourgeois notion of human dignity as an astigmatic delusion."[11] Perhaps so. But Maltz's faith in the "endurance of human dignity" was (as it remains today) a deeply held conviction that was as quintessential to his work as it was to his very existence. Maltz's belief in man's potential to do good cannot be denied him. More importantly, whether or not it is tender-minded, *The Cross and the Arrow* remains a richly dramatic story, one that well deserved the plaudits it received upon its publication.

V *What Shall We Ask of Writers?*

In the early part of 1946, a year after the publication of *The Cross and the Arrow*, Maltz became the focal point of a controversy which remains among the bitterest experiences of his life. During the summer of 1945 the editors of *New Masses,* together with several friends and contributors, met to discuss the work of the magazine. Shortly thereafter, in an article entitled "Probing Writers' Problems," one of the participants, Isidore Schneider, summarized the views he had offered at the discussions which had been concerned primarily with cultural matters.[12] In February, 1946, *New Masses* printed "What Shall We Ask of Writers?"[13] a response by Maltz to Schneider's article, which promptly set off a barrage of attacks against Maltz by several prominent writers of the Left Establishment.

The issue was an old one for the writers on the Left. It centered on the question of the writer's responsibility as a citizen-writer, and was in effect a variation on the question of whether art was to be used as a weapon in the class war. This was a matter which the Left had debated in the United States for more than twenty years and which, during the 1930s, had dominated the American Writers' Congress. Although there was never any agreement among left-wing writers on definitions — on what, for example, the very term "proletarian literature" actually meant — there was seldom disagreement on the role the artist had to assume. The artist, as Waldo Frank wrote in his Foreword to the published record of the first American Writers' Congress, had to form an alliance with the working class to combat the threat to their culture and very lives as creative men and women which was implicit in the capitalistic system; writers and artists were "held together by a common devotion to the need of building a new world from which the evils endangering mankind will have been uprooted, and in which the foundation will live for the creating of a universal human culture."[14] And, as Maltz was to tell a gathering of members of the West Coast Chapters of the League of American Writers in Los Angeles on March 10, 1943, the artist was in an unusual situation because his trade made him responsible to his fellow man. The writer himself might often be personally irresponsible, Maltz conceded; but, "This makes no difference. He is responsible none the less because society, humankind, holds him responsible." The artist must be the conscience of mankind: "This magnet, this great conscience of the world, the human cry for the right to realize man's potentialities on earth — this it has been the writers' privilege to express." Until the battle for complete human liberty, for the material foundation of human dignity, is won, Maltz concluded, "writers will have their place in the struggle of mankind and society."[15]

Isidore Schneider's article, which *New Masses* printed on October 23, 1945, offered nothing new; it was, as Daniel Aaron has described it, "a thoughtful and almost wistful" piece of writing which essentially repeated what "[Joseph] Freeman, [Michael] Gold, and [Stanley] Kunitz had been saying off and on for years."[16] According to Schneider, the writers who attended the meetings held by the editors of *New Masses* had reluctantly concluded that "no formulated Marxist criticism exists, serving as do Marx's *Capital,* Lenin's *State and Revolution,* or Stalin's *On the National Question* in their fields"; American Marxists therefore could strive, without feeling undue handicaps, "to win a socialist competition in the creation of a Marxist criticism.'' Indeed, Schneider continued, when Marxist principles are finally established in criticism, it is likely that their main lines will already have been drawn in social criticism of the Left.

Moreover, the impact of this criticism in its most influential period, the middle 1930s, was seen to come not from original contributions, but was in actuality a restatement "in more accurate Marxist terms, of the effects of the social environment, upon culture," which already had been noted by such bourgeois critics as Taine, Brandes, and Parrington. What gave the work of left-wing critics of the thirties its impact was their "enthusiasm, tenacity and their boldness in applying social criticism to current work"; to place a work within its social frame, Schneider contended, had consequently become an obligation of the critic. (At the same time, Schneider warned Left critics against being diverted from their main direction into culturally reactionary bypaths — a way of thinking, Schneider asserted, which has "led us to confine the brilliant work of a Kenneth Burke into an 'ivory tower' not of Burke's construction but a mirage of our own," as well as to dispose of the "vast contributions of James Joyce on the 'dung heap of decadence.' ")

Finally, it was the sense of those present at the *New Masses'* meetings that the recognition of the social role of the writer involved a recognition of his social responsibility; and that the safest authority for a writer to turn to was his own experience (for it was through "the reaction of labor audiences and the organizational or agitational work that he does, [that] the writer gradually defines his responsibilities to the labor movement"). Schneider acknowledged that this frequently caused the left-wing writer to oscillate between two poles: "At one the writer obliterates his literary self in the role of organizer... At the other is the obliteration of his labor affiliations with the writer withdrawing more and more until his participation is restricted to the occasional contribution of his signature." In addition, although almost all writers think in terms of work they hope will endure, most writers on the Left "find themselves writing for the moment — to report immediate events or to propagandize for immediate objectives." To report immediate events, Schneider contended, was an "honorable and useful function," as was the attempt to produce lasting works. What was harmful was to confuse the two, and that was what some writers on the Left had done: they "sought to solve a conflict of conscience by trying to do the two in one.'' However, this conflict became less problematic when the writer realized that he need not worry about his work being politically correct as long as his work was "faithful to reality.'' For one important aspect of Marxism was its facing up to reality, Schneider wrote in conclusion, and the Marxist writer could thus add to his advantages the fact that "his Marxist understanding enlarges his capacity to understand reality.''

Maltz's "What Shall We Ask of Writers?'' was not a refutation of Schneider's "frank and earnest article on writers' problems'' but an attempt to add to the discussion: "It has been my conclusion for some time,'' Maltz wrote, "that much of left wing artistic activity — both creative and critical — has been restricted, narrowed, turned away from life, sometimes made sterile — because the atmosphere and thinking of the literary left wing has been based upon a shallow approach.'' Schneider was correct in noting that left-wing writers were confused. But, although he recognized the problem, Schneider did not go on to uncover the deep source of it. *Most* left-wing writers were confused (not just a few, as Schneider had contended), and the reason they were, Maltz asserted, was that the "conflict of conscience,'' which results in wasted writing or bad art, *"has been induced in the writer by the intellectual atmosphere of the left wing.* The errors of individual writers or critics largely flow from a central source . . . That source is the vulgarization of the theory of art which lies behind left wing thinking: namely, 'art is a weapon.' ''

Maltz emphasized that "properly and broadly interpreted,'' he was in agreement with the doctrine that art was a weapon, for to the degree that works of art reflect or attack the values of whichever class holds the dominant social power, they have been or can be "weapons in man's thinking, and therefore in the struggle of social classes — either on the side of humanity's progress, or on the side of reaction.'' But as the Left wing in America had interpreted the doctrine "art is a weapon'' since 1930, it had become, Maltz contended, a hard rock of narrow thinking. The doctrine had come to be viewed as though it consisted only of the word "weapon''; the *nature* of art — how art may best be a weapon, and how it may not — had been slurred over. Consequently, Maltz wrote, "I have come to believe that the accepted understanding of art as a weapon is not a useful guide, but a straitjacket.'' From its originally profound insight, the doctrine of "art is a weapon'' had been turned into a vulgar slogan: art *should be* a weapon. In turn, this came to mean, "art should be a weapon as a leaflet is a weapon." And, finally, it has been understood in practice to mean that *"unless* art is a weapon like a leaflet, serving immediate political ends, necessities and programs, it is worthless or escapist or vicious."

The abuse of this doctrine, Maltz continued, resulted in the "constriction" and "stupidities" found all too often in "the earnest but narrow thinking and practice of the literary left." One result of this vulgarized approach was that creative writers had come to be judged primarily by this formal ideology; no matter how insightful or imaginative a work might be, if it seemed to imply "wrong" political conclusions it would be "indicted, severely mauled or beheaded — as the case may be." As an example, Maltz cited the case of Lillian Hellman's *Watch on the Rhine.* Produced as a play in 1940, *Watch on the Rhine* was attacked by the reviewer for *New Masses;* but two years later, when it appeared — unaltered — as a film, it was warmly praised by *New Masses.* The cause for this change in attitude was clear: "events had transpired in the two years calling for a different political program"; in neither review, however, was *Watch on the Rhine* discussed as a work of art.

And the opposite error, a corollary to his failure of Left criticism, was equally operative: praise, as well as prizes (to Clara Weatherwax's *Marching! Marching!,* for example), was frequently bestowed upon works which ten years later not even the critics for *New Masses* would bother to read. The situation for the left-wing writer thus seemed to Maltz to be insuperably difficult. Because the writer respected the tenets of Left criticism, he was confronted with the apparent obligation of writing both a novel and an editorial that would embrace all current political propositions which even remotely touched his material. And this, Maltz counseled, was not a method "by which art can be made rich, or the artist freed to do his most useful work."

Moreover, Maltz insisted, writers must be judged by their work and not by the committees they joined. An artist, as Engels had made clear in his appreciation of Balzac, could be a great artist without being an integrated or logical or progressive thinker on all matters. Thus, it was erroneous to assume (as many critics on the Left did) that a writer making a speech was performing the same act as writing a novel; it was imperative that literary critics appraise literary works only. To judge a writer solely by his personality or his political position would in many instances force the critics on the Left either to ignore or attack a writer whose politics was unacceptable to *New Masses*. This, Maltz noted, was exactly what happened with James T. Farrell, whose name had been a "bright pennant in the *New Masses* until he became hostile to the *New Masses*."

Maltz himself did not like the committees to which Farrell belonged, but he nevertheless regarded him as one of the outstanding writers in America. And this was true not only of Farrell, but of Richard Wright, Kenneth Fearing, and Lillian Smith, among others. Books, then, like new coins, have to be weighed in terms of what they are: no other standard is valid. For although a writer's political convictions *may* have something to do with either his growth or creative decline, this is not always so; and, Maltz argued, any assumption that there is a direct correlation between a writer's artistic stature and his political convictions "is the assumption of naiveté."

Finally, Maltz considered the specific effect which the doctrine "art is a weapon" had upon creative writing. The artist, he wrote, by the very nature of his craft, was able to show us people in motion; and the most successful artist was the one who "most profoundly and *accurately* reveals his characters, with all their motivations clearly delineated." But the writer who works to serve an immediate political purpose has set himself the task not of revealing men and society as they are but of "grinding a tactical axe. And this misuse of art, this tendency of the left-wing artist to practice journalism instead of art, results in shallow writing which is neither the best journalism, nor the best art, *nor* the best politics."

It was this crucial failure of Left writing which provoked Maltz to conclude "What Shall We Ask of Writers?" with a warning to the creative artists on the Left. It was not incumbent upon them, Maltz wrote, to relate their philosophical or emotional humanism to a current and transient political tactic. But, if the individual writer chooses to do so, "he must remember that, where art is a weapon, it is only so when it is art. Those artists who work within a vulgarized approach to art do so at great peril to their own work and to the very purpose they seek to serve."

The response to Maltz's article by the Left Establishment was as immediate as it was harsh. It began rather mildly with an article by Schneider in the same issue of *New Masses* in which "What Shall We Ask of Writers?" appeared. Schneider, entitling his article "Background to Error,"[17] was content to direct himself to two areas of Maltz's discussion, one of which he felt remained "dim," while the other had been left "blank." The dim area was that of the achievement of left-wing criticism which, Schneider contended, was "considerable in lasting effects though not in lasting works." The more significant failure of Maltz's contribution to the discussion of left-wing writing — the area which Maltz had left blank — was the historical background to the present state of Left writing. Schneider conceded that the result of the struggle for an American Marxist criticism was not what he or any left-wing critic had willed. But, he argued, it was comparatively easy to acknowledge errors and make resolutions to reform, just as it was "dangerously easy to 'correct' the error in the old-fashioned way of a plunge into opposite error." The difficult but necessary thing to do was to analyze the error (which could only be done by an accompanying analysis of the social context of the error), for it was only by understanding what had already occurred — what difficulties the Left had already faced — that the left-wing writer would be able to bring about effects closer to the will of the Left in their struggle to establish a Marxist criticism in America.

In the weeks following the simultaneous publication of "What Shall We Ask of Writers?" and "Background to Error," Maltz was subjected to the severest attack the literary Left had leveled against any writer since it had ceased flogging Archibald MacLeish.[18] Howard Fast, for example, criticized Maltz for charting a road that led to sterility, "whether it be the sterility of the esthete, the mediocrity, or the neo-fascist." To ask that a writer divorce himself from politics, Fast wrote, is to ask that he exile himself from civilization; and, consequently, the end product of Maltz's direction would be liquidation — "not only of Marxist creative writing — but of all creative writing which bases itself on progressive currents in America."[19] Joseph North, writing in the same issue of *New Masses* as Fast, continued the attack by warning that there was "no Retreat for the Writer."[20] Maltz, he stated, had departed from that principal contention of the Left, postulated by Lenin, which declared that "Literature must become a part of the proletarian cause as a whole." Were Maltz's counsel to be heeded, it would destroy the fruitful tree of Marxism; clearly then, North snapped, Maltz's position was destructively anti-Marxist.

Alvah Bessie further contributed to the onslaught by posing the question, "What Is Freedom for Writers?"[21] The answer was that the Left needed something more than "free" artists. What was needed was *Party* artists, artists who were "deeply, truly and honestly rooted in the working class who realized the truth of

Lenin's assertion that the absolute freedom they seek 'is nothing but a bourgeois or anarchist phrase... It is impossible to live in a society and yet be free from it. The freedom of the bourgeois writer, artist, or actress is nothing but a self-destructive (or hypocritically deceiving) dependence upon the money bags, upon bribery, upon patronage.' '' What was needed was writers who would joyfully impose upon themselves the discipline of understanding and acting upon working-class theory; only such writers, Bessie insisted, would be able to create a truly free literature because only these writers would serve the tens of millions of workers who are the strength of the country. "This is what we shall ask of writers," Bessie concluded. "And in time we will get it." John Lawson's response, "Art Is a Weapon,"[22] was similar to Bessie's, only Lawson's authority was Marx rather than Lenin: Marx, Lawson asserted, "says that 'Theory becomes a material force as soon as it has gripped the masses.' This is true of all thought and of all imaginative and creative activity. It is another way of saying that art is a weapon."

On April 9, 1946, less than a month after the appearance of Lawson's article, *New Masses* published Maltz's statement of self-castigation, "Moving Forward": "I consider now [Maltz wrote] that my article — by what I have come to agree was a one-sided, non-dialectical treatment of complex issues — could not, as I had hoped, have contributed to the development of left-wing criticism and creative writing. I believe also that my critics were entirely correct in insisting that certain fundamental ideas in my article would, if pursued to their conclusion, result in the dissolution of the left-wing cultural movement."[23] Maltz conceded that his article had bristled with errors; that, most importantly, as Samuel Sillen had noted in the *Daily Worker,* "What Shall We Ask of Writers?" was an example of revisionist thinking in the cultural field — and revisionism was most responsible for the gradual sapping of the literary Left's Marxist base. So, recanting his praise of the likes of James Farrell, and apologizing for unwittingly giving such magazines as *The New Leader* support in their "unprincipled slanders against the Left," Maltz reaffirmed his faith in Marxism:

If the writer is to retain inner firmness, if he is not to sink into cynicism and despair, if he is to maintain his love for people, without which true art cannot flourish, then he must understand that events have a meaning, that history has a direction, that the characters he portrays are part of a social web based upon the life and death struggle of class. For this understanding, for inner firmness, for the spiritual ability to retain faith in people and faith in the future, he must, in this epoch, turn to Marxism.

A few days after the publication of "Moving Forward," the *Daily Worker* and *New Masses* held a symposium on "Art Is a Weapon." Maltz did not attend the forum, which was held in New York, but he sent a message from Hollywood in which he again committed himself to the principles of "Moving Forward": "The cultural contribution of the artist," Maltz wrote in part, "is direct and immediate, and it can be weighed. He must decide the cultural tradition he wishes to serve: A dying culture founded on privilege, or the rising culture of the people, that will be founded on economic and social equality. He must speak for one or the other, find his roots in one or the other."[24]

With this statement Maltz withdrew from the controversy. He had been forced into an untenable position, and to this day he prefers not to discuss the matter. But it is just for his part in this controversy (together with the events surrounding The Hollywood Ten episode) that he is most often remembered. And the accounts of his role in the controversy have not been favorable. Most literary and social historians regard his position as a rather shameful one, and they have frequently described it in unsympathetic and even contemptuous terms. In *The Radical Novel in the United States,* for example, Walter Rideout wrote that Maltz had repudiated the "latitudinarian arguments of ['What Shall We Ask of Writers?'] under the most humiliating conditions, but he presumably did not also repudiate his memory";[25] Daniel Aaron, in his study of the *Writers on the Left,* similarly commented that Maltz had "suffered a serious ideological collapse but was nursed back to regularity by solicitous comrades";[26] and David Shannon, in his biased and often ridiculous *Decline of American Communism: A History of the Communist Party in the United States Since 1945,* offered the observation that Maltz neither stood firm nor defied the attacks of his friends and the Party leadership: "He recanted, utterly and abjectly. He crawled."[27]

Although Aaron, Rideout, and Shannon are accurate in their presentation of the basic facts of the episode, they make no attempt to explain the significance of this *cause célèbre,* nor do they attempt to understand Maltz himself. It has remained for George Charney, a former chairman of the New York Communist Party and a mem-

ber of the Party's national committee, to begin at least to put the
episode into meaningful perspective. In his memoir, *A Long
Journey,* published ten years after his resignation from the Party,
Charney recalls that he knew Maltz in the 1930s and regarded him
as a man of integrity and talent who was dedicated to the fight
against fascism.[28] "He was a quiet and unassuming man," Charney
writes, "with a profound respect for the political leaders of the
movement and thought only in terms of how he could modestly
serve as a writer." His challenge to the sacred shibboleth of "art is
a weapon" thus took the Left completely by surprise, which no
doubt accounted for the withering attack launched against Maltz
not only by the "timeservers" in the cultural group but by national
leaders of the Party who regarded "What Shall We Ask of
Writers?" as "dramatic proof of the insidious influences on the
arts that 'infiltrated' the movement." For Charney, the importance
of this episode is not that Maltz felt compelled to denounce his own
cogent arguments against the misuse of the doctrine that art is a
weapon, but that "it dramatized the resurgent spirit of reconstitu-
tion and the hard uncompromising attitude toward liberalism and
dissent, especially in the cultural periphery of the movement."

That the Left was taken by surprise by "What Shall We Ask of
Writers?" is clear from their response to the article; equally apparent is the disdain which literary and social historians have for what
they regard as Maltz's capitulation to the Communist Party in
"Moving Forward." Yet both attitudes arise from a profound failure to confront the complexities of Maltz's commitments; a failure,
that is, to recognize that from his very first work Maltz was torn
between a commitment to the dreams of the Left and to the often
conflicting demands of his artistic sensibility. In the thirties, few
writers on the Left were Maltz's equal; and, as Alfred Kazin had
noted in *On Native Grounds,* "Of the host of younger writers who
seemed to promise so much to Marxist critics in the early thirties —
the Tillie Lerners, the Arnold Armstrongs, the Ben Fields — only
Richard Wright and Albert Maltz went on writing at all."[29] Wright,
of course, finally broke with the Left; Maltz did not and could not.
Despite the events in Europe that were causing many intellectuals to
break with the Left, Maltz continued to believe that the social
injustices of America could only be changed by radical means: his
commitment to Marxism and the dream of a new world remained
as strong as ever. But so, too, did his belief that a writer had to be
concerned with his art. And as he reaffirmed his political commit-

ment to the right against Fascism, racism, and imperialism, he also continued to study the prose styles of his literary idols, John Galsworthy, Liam O'Flaherty, and André Malraux.

No doubt Maltz was more than a little naive to believe in the mid-forties that the Soviet Union of Joseph Stalin would become anything but a totalitarian state; and we may well wonder just how much Maltz allowed his literary talents to be stunted by his attempts to accommodate his artistic imagination to his political and social concerns. But that he chose to publicly repudiate the aesthetic concerns he set forth in "What Shall We Ask of Writers?" for a total commitment to a system that we can now recognize for all its weaknesses and failures (yet which for Maltz was the only hope for a decaying society) is deserving not of the snide judgments which some historians have indulged in but of an understanding of the enormous pressures which the immediacy of the political situation exerted upon him and which, because of the choice he felt compelled to make, has caused him considerable anguish.

VI   *The Hollywood Ten*

Before the furor over "What Shall We Ask of Writers?" had subsided, the federal government embarked upon its policy of harassing people in the movie industry whose political affiliations they considered to be suspect, and Maltz suddenly found himself among the focal figures in yet another (and even uglier) controversy. Although the House Committee on Un-American Activities (HUAC) did not begin its hearings on the subversive elements in Hollywood until 1947, the witch hunt had been gestating for a long time. As early as 1938, Martin Dies had intended to investigate the Communist "takeover" of the motion picture industry but never quite got started; that feat remained for the less well-known but equally insidious John E. Rankin. It was Rankin who proposed on January 3, 1945, the opening day of the seventy-ninth Congress, that the Committee on Un-American Activities not only be made a standing committee of the House but that its investigative scope and power be greatly increased. By a vote of 207 to 186, Congress gave its approval, and that was the start. By June, Rankin was "on the trail of the tarantula"; his Committee was ready to send investigators to Hollywood — "the greatest hotbed of subversive activities in America" — where they were prepared to uncover "one of the most dangerous plots ever instigated for the overthrow of the government." Rankin needed no other evidence than the fact that a large number of Jews were working in Hollywood at the time, for, as Walter Goodman has commented in his study of *The Committee,* "In Rankin's mind, to call a Jew a Communist was a tautology."[30]

Nevertheless, the investigation was slow in developing; there were too many other subversive activities and organizations operating in America for the Committee to give all its attention to the Hollywood tarantulas. But by 1947 the Committee was ready, and under the chairmanship of J. Parnell Thomas, the anti-New Dealer who had supplanted the raucous John Rankin as the most powerful member of HUAC, the purge of Hollywood "subversives" got under way. A closed preliminary hearing was held in May, and fourteen witnesses — all friendly to the Committee — were called. Adolphe Menjou told the Committee members that "Hollywood is one of the main centers of Communist activity in America"; the mother of actress Ginger Rogers reported that in Dalton Trumbo's film, *Tender Comrade,* her daughter had been asked (and refused) to speak the line, "Share and share alike — that's democracy"; and Robert Taylor related that he had been prevented from entering the Navy until he had finished filming *Song of Russia.*[31] The Committee was satisfied: an indictment was issued, and on September 23, 1947, forty-five people in the motion picture industry were subpoenaed to appear before the House Committee on Un-American Activities. One month later, on October 20, the Hollywood hearings began; they were, as one historian has noted, "the most flamboyant and widely publicized hearings" in the Committee's history.[32]

With J. Parnell Thomas as its spokesman, the Committee (which also consisted of Richard B. Vail, John McDowell, and Richard M. Nixon) made it known that they expected the hearings to prove that Communists had infiltrated the motion picture industry, that they had in fact succeeded in putting subersive propaganda into various films, and that "the White House exerted its influence on certain people to have pro-Russian motion pictures filmed during the regime of President Roosevelt." (Thomas clearly was determined to link the New Deal and Communism; on June 6, 1947, for example, he read into the *Congressional Record* the subcommittee's contention that "some of the most flagrant communist propaganda films were produced as the result of White House pressure.")[33] To achieve their end, the Committee began by calling upon a host of

"friendly" witnesses, many of whom had testified at the preliminary hearings in California. Gary Cooper took the stand to
denounce Communism because "From what I hear, I don't like it
because it isn't on the level"; Lela Rogers once again reported that
she turned down several un-American scripts which had been
offered her daughter, the most notable being the screenplay of
Theodore Dreiser's *Sister Carrie,* which Mrs. Rogers regarded as
"just as open propaganda as 'None But the Lonely Heart' '"; Ayn
Rand, who had not as yet written *The Fountainhead,* attacked
Song of Russia as a blatantly propagandistic film because it
depicted several Russians who were smiling and Russians no longer
smiled, Miss Rand told the Committee, or "If they do [smile], it is
privately and accidentally. Certainly, it is not social. They don't
smile in approval of their system"; and Adolphe Menjou informed
the Committee that he would "move to the State of Texas if [Com-
munism] ever came here because I think the Texans would kill them
on sight."[34]

The testimony of Messrs. Cooper and Menjou, Miss Rand, and
Mrs. Rogers, as well as such other friendly witnesses as Jack L.
Warner, Louis B. Mayer, Walt Disney, Robert Taylor, Sam Wood,
and Leo McCarey dominated the first week of the hearings. The
second week was devoted to testimony by the accused. Nineteen
Hollywood figures had been subpoenaed, but only eleven were
actually called to give testimony. And only one of the eleven,
Bertolt Brecht, chose to respond directly to the Committee's basic
question: "Are you now or have you ever been a member of the
Communist Party?" Brecht appeared on the ninth and final day of
the hearings (October 30), and no doubt was expected to be an unfriendly witness. (The Committee's interest in Brecht apparently
was the result of the dramatist's collaborations with composer
Hanns Eisler, the younger brother of Gerhardt and a member of
the International Music Bureau.[35]) But Brecht confounded the
Committee by remarking that as a guest of the United States he did
not want to enter into any legal arguments and quite simply stated
that he had never been a member of the Communist Party, either in
the United States or in Germany.[36] The remaining witnesses —
Alvah Bessie, Herbert Biberman, Lester Cole, Edward Dmytryk,
Ring Lardner, Jr., John Howard Lawson, Albert Maltz, Samuel
Ornitz, Adrian Scott, and Dalton Trumbo — refused to respond
directly to the question of their political affiliation, contending that
the question violated the First Amendment, and consequently they

became known as The Unfriendly Ten and then as The Hollywood Ten.[37]

The Hollywood Ten did not, in fact, actually refuse to answer the question of their trade union and political affiliations; they merely failed to do so. As Alvah Bessie was to write almost twenty years later in *Inquisition in Eden*: "We had been more than willing to talk, but the Committee was not interested in the point of testimony we were anxious to adduce. Our point was that the Committee itself was unconstitutional, since it could not legislate in the field of ideas, opinions, or associations."[38] And it was precisely this point that the first of the "unfriendly witnesses," John Howard Lawson, argued. "I am not on trial here, Mr. Chairman," Lawson told Thomas. "This Committee is on trial before the American people. Let us get that straight." When Thomas asked the usual question about the defendant's political affiliation, Lawson replied, "The question of Communism is in no way related to this inquiry, which is an attempt to get control of the screen and to invade the basic right of American citizens in all fields." As Thomas began to pound his gavel, Lawson continued: "The question here relates not only to the question of my membership in any political organization, but this Committee is attempting to establish the right which has been historically denied to any committee of this sort, to invade the rights and privileges and immunity of American citizens, whether they be Protestant, Methodist, Jewish or Catholic; whether they be Republicans, Democrats, or anything else."[39] Lawson adamantly refused to say whether he was a member of the Communist Party, and on October 27 was cited for contempt of Congress. So, too, was the next defendant, Dalton Trumbo, who, according to Thomas, "followed the usual Communist line of not responding to questions of the Committee," thereby offering "definite proof that he is a member of the Communist Party."[40]

Maltz was next. Earlier in the year, in an address delivered at a Conference on Thought Control in the United States, Maltz had excoriated the Un-American Activities Committee for its harassment of the Executive Board of the Joint Anti-Fascist Committee. In the Committee's citation against novelist Howard Fast, Maltz had told the conference in a speech which he entitled "The Writer as Conscience of the People," that "the shadow of Rankin has fallen across the desk of every other American writer." And, he warned, it will not leave of its own accord: "when individuals who are the political scum of our nation are seated in Congress, and are given the power to intimidate decent citizens,'' the time has come ''for honest men and women of letters in America to spring to awareness.''[41] With his disgust for the Committee's very existence having been so strongly expressed just three months before his own hearing, Maltz expected the same treatment as John Lawson and Dalton Trumbo.

Both Lawson and Trumbo had attempted to have written statements read to the Committee, and both had been refused permission (though, as Trumbo wryly noted, the Committee did not hesitate to hear a prepared statement from Gerald L. K. Smith).[42] It was somewhat of a shock, therefore, when the Committee agreed to allow Maltz to read his statement. To be sure, the Committee did insist on first examining the statement; and, as Maltz noted, they had not asked Smith to submit *his* statement for their approval. Yet it is all the more surprising that the Committee, having perused Maltz's prepared comments, permitted him to read the statement. For it was a devastating attack on the Committee, and Maltz was to make the most of his opportunity.

The House Committee on Un-American Activities, Maltz declared, had denied to him and several others the right to cross-examine the well-rehearsed witnesses who had appeared during the first week of the hearings and in fact had granted congressional immunity to these witnesses so that they could not be sued for libel. This procedure, Maltz asserted, was not only evil and vicious, but legally unjust and morally indecent; it ''places in danger every other American, since if the right of any one citizen can be invaded, then the constitutional guarantees of every other American have been subverted and no one is any longer protected from official tyranny.'' And if the Committee does have the right to brand who and what is un-American, then ''who is ultimately safe from this Committee except for members of the Ku Klux Klan?''

Maltz went on to suggest that one of the reasons he had been commanded to appear before the Committee was his support of the New Deal which, according to the official transcript, Representative Thomas believed was ''working hand in glove with the Communist Party.'' But it was not only on the policies of the New Deal that Maltz and the Committee disagreed: ''In common with many Americans,'' Maltz said, ''I supported, against Mr. Thomas and Mr. Rankin, the anti-lynching bill. I opposed them in my support of OPA controls and emergency veteran housing and a fair employment practices law.'' And he now opposed the Committee in their attempt to prevent him from thinking and speaking freely:

I insist upon my right [Maltz told the Committee] . . . to join the Republican Party or the Communist Party, the Democratic or the Prohibition Party; to publish whatever I please; to fix my mind or change my mind, without dictation from anyone; to offer any criticism I think fitting of any public official or policy; to join whatever organizations I please, no matter what legislators may think of them. Above all, I challenge the right of this Committee to inquire into my political or religious beliefs, in any manner or degree, and I assert that not only the conduct of the Committee but its very existence are a subversion of the Bill of Rights.

The American people are going to have to choose between the Bill of Rights and the Un-American Activities Committee, Maltz concluded his statement. "They cannot have both. One or the other must be abolished in the immediate future."[43]

After he finished reading his statement, Maltz was asked the usual questions: Was he a member of the Screen Writers' Guild? Was he a member of the Communist Party? When he refused to answer yes or no, Thomas responded in his usual way, "Excuse the witness. No more questions. Typical Communist line." Two days and seven more unfriendly witnesses later, the hearings on what Max Lerner referred to as the attempt "to track down the footprints of Karl Marx in movieland"[44] came to an abrupt end with Thomas's announcement that that days' hearings concluded the first phase of the Committee's investigation of Communism in the motion picture industry. Ten prominent Hollywood figures had refused to deny that they were members of the Communist Party, Thomas noted, and he adjourned the hearings with the ominous comment that "It is not necessary for the Chair to emphasize the harm which the motion-picture industry suffers from the presence within its rank of known Communists who do not have the best interest of the United States at heart. The industry should set about immediately to clean its own house and not wait for public opinion to force it to do so."[45]

From the outset, there had been cries of protest against the hearings. The Committee was condemned in newspaper editorials; as early as the third week of October a Committee for the First Amendment was formed with the support of such Hollywood luminaries as Robert Ryan, Edward G. Robinson, Danny Kaye, and Sterling Hayden. A newspaper and radio campaign was undertaken (on one of the programs, "Hollywood Fights Back," Thomas Mann said: "I have the honor to expose myself as a hostile witness. . . . As an American citizen of German birth, I finally testify that I am painfully familiar with certain political trends. Spiritual intolerance, political inquisitions, and declining legal security, and all this in the name of an alleged 'state of emergency' . . . that is how it started in Germany. What followed was fascism, and what followed fascism was war.'').[46] A plane called "Star of the Red Sea" made a well-publicized flight to Washington to protest the hearings; and, on October 29, twenty-eight members of The Committee for the First Amendment presented a petition to Congress on behalf of more than five hundred public figures "for redress of our grievances."[47]

Nevertheless, on November 26, 1947, less than a month after Representative Thomas had admonished the movie industry to "clean its own house," the *New York Times* reported that at a secret meeting of fifty motion picture executives, the Hollywood moguls had unanimously agreed to "discharge or suspend [The Hollywood Ten] without compensation," and would not rehire any of them until they declared under oath that they were not Communists. [48] Two days later RKO fired Adrian Scott and Edward Dmytryk; on November 30, 20th Century-Fox fired Ring Lardner, Jr.; and on December 1, Lester Cole and Dalton Trumbo were suspended without pay. John Howard Lawson, Alvah Bessie, Herbert Biberman, Samuel Ornitz, and Albert Maltz were not under contract at the time, so they could not be fired or "suspended"; they were simply placed on an open blacklist.

On April 24, two days before the Motion Picture Association of America was to meet in New York at the Waldorf-Astoria Hotel to give its unanimous approval to a Hollywood blacklist, the citations against The Hollywood Ten were brought before a special session of Congress. In part, the session had been called for the purpose of allocating funds to resist the spread of Communism in Europe, and the members of the Committee decided to use the occasion to launch a verbal onslaught against the Ten.[49] And Maltz, who was the first on the list for contempt citation, bore the brunt of the Committee's wrathful rhetoric. Representative McDowell began by reading a list of countries which had fallen to the Communists, and then informed the Congress that Maltz was a "colonel in the conspiratorial policy of Soviet Russia."[50] The citation against Maltz had been called first, McDowell announced, "because this man was the most arrogant, the most contemptible, the most bitter of all of these people who do not believe in their own country." McDowell continued his verbal assault on Maltz (as Gordon Kahn has commented) as though there had been a blood-feud between the Maltzs and McDowells for many generations.[51] Within a few minutes of McDowell's telling the Speaker that "Sometimes ... one wonders if public service and love of country, with all its great magnitude, is sufficient pull to retain membership or employment on this difficult Congressional assignment," the question was called, and by a vote of 347 to 17 Albert Maltz was cited for contempt of Congress and ordered turned over to the federal authorities.

The proceedings then continued in rapid order. Several members of the Congress — most notably Helen Gahagan Douglas, Vito Marcantonio, Jacob Javits, and Emanuel Celler (who announced that he was opposed to "even a little totalitarianism to preserve our democracy") — argued against the Committee's conduct, but they were strongly rebuked by the representative voices of John Rankin and Karl Mundt. Rankin, perhaps annoyed that he had not been on the Hollywood subcommittee, used this occasion to indulge once again in some Jew-Red-baiting. He noted that the petition sent to Congress by The Committee for the First Amendment had been signed by such personalities as Eddie Cantor and Melvyn Douglas, whose real names, Rankin felt compelled to point out, were Eddie Iskowitz and Melvyn Hesselber. There were others, "too numerous to mention," all of whom were "attacking the Committee for doing its duty in trying to protect this country and save the American people from the horrible fate that Communists have meted out to unfortunate Christian people in Europe."[52] And so it went. Before the afternoon was over, all of The Hollywood Ten had been cited for contempt.

The Ten, of course, had expected to be cited for contempt and, to some extent, wanted to be so cited. Their decision to stand on the First Amendment had been a deliberate choice, since they did have the option of taking the Fifth Amendment or to respond with a simple yes or no to the questions asked by the Committee. Once subpoenaed, however, the Ten decided to attempt to bring the Committee itself to court. The expectation, at least on the part of some defendants, was that the citations would eventually be appealed to the Supreme Court, and the Court would vote 5-4 in favor of the Ten.[53] What happened in fact was somewhat different: the Committee was indeed reviled and ridiculed — "The Hollywood investigation has been producing a good deal of nonsense and very little else," the *New York Herald Tribune* commented on November 1, 1947,[54] and J. Parnell Thomas was himself imprisoned in 1949 for having put some of his relatives on the public payroll and then accepting kickbacks from them — but the conviction of The Hollywood Ten was not overturned. Herbert Biberman and Edward Dmytryk were sentenced to six months in prison and fined $1,000; the others were given a year's sentence and the same fine. The convictions were appealed by John Howard Lawson and Dalton Trumbo on behalf of the entire group, but in 1949 the U.S. Court of Appeals upheld the convictions, stating that there was not the slightest doubt that "the Committee was and is constitutionally created, that it functions under valid statute and resolution which have repeatedly and without exception been upheld as constitutional, that the 'question under inquiry' by the Committee was proper, that the power of inquiry includes power to require a witness before the Committee to disclose whether or not he is a Communist, and the failure or refusal of a witness so to disclose is properly punishable...."[55]

Shortly after the Court rendered its decision, Maltz addressed a rally for Civil and Human Rights held in Madison Square Garden. He told the gathering that when the appeals of Lawson and Trumbo went to the Supreme Court, the issue in reality would be censorship; not only was the freedom of political association of the cultural world of America on appeal, but so was the ultimate freedom of all forms of expression.[56] For a while, Maltz was convinced that the Supreme Court would overrule the U.S. Court of Appeals. But the death of two of the Justices changed the balance of the Court, and it soon became clear that the convictions would be upheld. On April 23, 1950, Maltz addressed another rally, this one in Los Angeles, and angrily rebuked the system that was about to send him to prison. "I do not like the idea of spending a year of my life in a Federal prison," he began. But circumstances being what they were, "If the opportunity were offered ten times over, I would not withdraw a word, alter a sentence, change a tone of what I said before the unspeakable Committee on un-American activities — except where I could make the words sharper, the sentences more biting. And if we go to prison, I for one will go with a deeper anger than I ever have felt in my life."[57] In June, the Supreme Court announced that it was denying certiorari — Justices Douglas and Black dissenting with the majority decision — and The Hollywood Ten began to serve their prison terms for contempt of the committee which former President Truman once referred to as "the most un-American thing in America."

CHAPTER 7

"The Path of Man"

L ESS than a year before the Hollywood hearings were to begin, Maltz was asked to do some emergency screenwork on a film that was shooting on location about 150 miles north of Los Angeles. He spent a week on the project, then began the trip back to his home in Los Angeles. He drove through the San Joaquin Valley, and along the way stopped in a small town to pick up an old man, William Stevenson, who was trying to hitch a ride. As Stevenson picked up his coat and suitcase, Maltz saw that he could cover little more than six inches with each step he took. And when he reached the car it was apparent that he would not be able to get in without help. Maltz told Stevenson to try it "ass backwards," to "push in behind first." The old man turned around and, as Maltz was to write later, "His body began to tremble with nervousness. He sat down on the edge of the seat. His lips tightened into a hard line. Laboriously, straining, he inched his rump back toward the wheel of the car, farther and farther back until he was sitting behind the wheel itself. And then, his face creased with anxiety, he slowly began to swing his long legs into the car, using his hands to guide them, bending them at the knees as much as possible. There was an inch or two to spare."[1] So began what was to become *The Journey of Simon McKeever.*

As they drove, Stevenson told Maltz about himself. He had been born in Ireland in 1863, and some time in the early 1900s had "just walked across the bridge into the United States."[2] He apparently had taken out his first citizenship papers on several occasions, but because of the itinerant nature of his work (which kept him moving from "oil field to oil field and from one type of job to another") he had never become a citizen. He presently was making his way to Glendale, a suburb of Los Angeles, where he hoped to locate a woman physician who he had been told had a "miracle injection" that could cure him of the arthritis which had finally forced him, at the age of seventy-six, to stop working. His unemployment had resulted in his being placed in the County Poorhouse, and because he was afraid that he would not be allowed to leave the home of his own will, Stevenson informed Maltz, he had slipped away from the poorhouse with just enough money to get him to the county line. Despite his crippling arthritis, his lack of money, and his age, Stevenson was determined to get to Glendale; he was confident that the miracle injection would cure him of his infirmity and that he would be able to go back to work. Indeed, he wanted to see the doctor that very day, he told Maltz; there had already been too many empty tomorrows for him. So Maltz drove throughout the day and into the early evening; but by the time they reached Glendale it was too late for Stevenson to go to the doctor's office. Maltz drove him to a nearby motel, gave him money for a room and a few meals, and left. As far as he knew, that was to be the end of their association.

I   The Poorhouse

At the time of his encounter with Stevenson, Maltz had been doing some preparatory work on a novel and planned to continue with his project upon his return to Los Angeles. But in the days that followed the drive to Glendale, he found himself thinking of Stevenson so often that he finally decided to interrupt his work on the novel (which he never did get to write) and to try instead to write a short story about the old man. What most fascinated Maltz about Stevenson was "the man's extraordinary spirit — his zest for life, his interest in everything that was happening around in the world, his lively memories of the trade union struggles, his contact with the Wobblies, his sense of humor and, of course, his casual courage in doing what he was doing. He was a man with such a 'yea-saying' feeling about life that [Maltz] found him one of the most exhilarating persons with whom [he] had ever had contact." In the course of plotting the short story, Maltz's fascination with his subject grew even stronger, and before long he realized that his short story would have to be a short novel. Indeed, so intrigued had he become with the tenacious old man he had met on the road that Maltz finally decided to put off his other projects entirely and immediately set to work on his newly conceived novel.

As a starting point, Maltz went back up the San Joaquin Valley to Sacramento in order to take a look at the County Poorhouse in which Stevenson had been living and to map out the countryside through which the character he was to call Simon McKeever would do his hitch-hiking. Along the way Maltz also visited several privately run homes for elderly people, and from these visits came the Finney Home described in *The Journey of Simon McKeever*. When Maltz finally arrived at the poorhouse itself, he was surprised to find a rather attractive building which had been built during the WPA days. But inside the building, Maltz recalls, "all was as dreary and desolate as anything that could be imagined. There was a number of very large barrack-type rooms in which there was no room for anything but cots and footlockers. Man after man lay on lumpy straw sacking and stared vacantly at the ceiling."[3] No one seemed to know anything about Stevenson, and Maltz was preparing to leave when he accidentally found an employee who did remember the old man. Stevenson apparently had been taken to the County Hospital, where some hours later Maltz found him awaking from a prostate operation. More than a month had passed since the two had met, but Stevenson immediately recognized Maltz and told him that he had indeed seen the Glendale doctor, who had informed him that he had "degenerative arthritis"; a disease, she told him, that elderly people get, "particularly laborers or mechanics who have been kept using certain joints in their work over many years. It also seems to affect those who have been exposed to the weather through outdoor work . . . And there's no cure for it."[4]

From that point on, Maltz kept in contact with Stevenson, who was put in a section of the County Hospital reserved for those who are elderly and in need of medical care. Each month Maltz would send him money for pipe tobacco and other sundries, but he did not tell Stevenson that he was writing a book about him. As it was, work on the novel progressed more slowly than Maltz had anticipated. First there were various personal problems that prevented him from giving the novel his complete attention, and in October, 1947, he was subpoenaed for the hearings in Washington. By the end of the following year, however, the novel was finished, and in the spring of 1949 *The Journey of Simon McKeever* was published by Little, Brown and Company. It was the last time to date that a novel by Maltz appeared under the imprint of a major American publishing house.

II   *A Chance of Survival*

Many of the external elements of *The Journey of Simon*

McKeever are a literal rendering of the actual events. However, Maltz deliberately chose to fictionalize certain facts. Simon McKeever, for example, is ten years younger than his prototype, William Stevenson, was at the time. (Maltz was convinced that "some readers would not believe the story if I gave [Stevenson's] actual age.") More importantly, since Stevenson never became a United States citizen he was not a recipient of Social Security — as is Simon McKeever — and as a result he became a resident of the County Poorhouse in Sacramento. Maltz decided to change this in the novel because he wanted his character "to be more representative of that section of our society which is beyond 65 and subsists on old age insurance, and which does not reside in a city or county run home but in the kind of private establishment run for profit."[5] Despite the social concern, however, *The Journey of Simon McKeever* is the least political of Maltz's novels. Ten years earlier, in "Hotel Raleigh, the Bowery," Maltz had used a similar setting to excoriate American society. But for all the parallels between the Hotel Raleigh and the Finney Home, between the bottom dogs of the 1937 novella and the elderly inhabitants of the Home, it is neither the slow, painful death of a Jimmy O'Shaughnessy nor the men who keep "talkin' pie in the sky while [they] got wind in [their] belly" that is of primary importance to Maltz in *Simon McKeever.* It is Simon's "extraordinary spirit," his "yea-saying feeling about life," that dominates the novel and insists, as William Du Bois wrote, "that man the individual has at least an outside chance of survival."[6]

III   *The Path of Man*

When *The Journey of Simon McKeever* was published, several reviewers referred to it is a modern *Pilgrim's Progress.*[7] The analogy is certainly apt, but it is the influence of Maxim Gorki and Franz Kafka rather than John Bunyan that is most felt throughout *Simon McKeever.* Maltz prefaces his novel with a quotation from Gorki's *Lower Depths:* "What is a man [asks Satin]? He is not you, not I, not they ... no! He is you, I, they, the old man, Napoleon, Mohammed — all in one! Do you understand? That's tremendous. In that are — all beginnings and all endings. All is in man, all is for man! Only man exists, everything else — is the work of his hand and his brain. Man! That is — magnificent! There's such pride in the word! M-A-N! You must respect man! Not pity him ... not lower him with pity . . . you must value him! Let's drink to man, Baron!'' There is another view of man, however, one which haunts the aging Simon McKeever whenever he tries to sleep. The night-mare is always the same: "he [Simon] was on a road — a car came — he tried to move — and he was run down like a cockroach and squashed; then, most distressing of all, people stood around examining the remains and said: "Why — he was only a cockroach after all; not a man, a bug." Simon must decide if he is a man or a bug; he must decide if there is in fact any difference between the one and the other. And, indirectly, he must also decide if the lines from Gorki's play are only the self-deluding comments of a half-drunken criminal or if Satin is right in saying that man is free, "that he is born for something better to come." The journey even-tually provides Simon with the answers.

It is only by accident that Simon even begins his journey. He finds a twenty-five cent piece in the street, and immediately goes to a nearby drugstore to buy some tobacco. At the Thomas Finney Rest Home, where he is residing as an old age pensioner of the state, Simon is given a weekly allotment of tobacco, but it is nothing more than "a weekly ration of horse manure or mattress sweepings or whatever else the poetry of the old man's bitterness might choose to call it." And since all of his fifty-five-dollar-a-month insurance money is turned over to the Finneys to cover the cost of board and lodgings, Simon has long gone without a can of good tobacco. Thus, when the clerk in the drugstore cannot supply him with a tin of Leslie Plug, he gladly settles for two cans of Half and Half. With his purchase securely tucked away in his pocket, Simon contentedly though laboriously begins to make his way toward the door; only then does he become aware of the squat, unattractive woman who has been staring at him. As he moves along, the woman's scrutiny continues and finally becomes too impertinent for Simon to accept in silence; if there was one thing he resented, "it was to be stared at as though his lameness made him a freak." Sourly, out of the corner of his mouth, he says to the woman, "Take a good look, young lady, won't cost you a cent." Her reply is a burst of laughter that leaves Simon bristling with anger. But before he can say anything, the woman comes toward him and in a warm, sympathetic voice apologizes. She had not meant to embarrass him, she tells Simon; she had just been wonder-ing "how long you've had arthritis, you poor man."

Simon is bewildered. He wants to know how she knows he has

arthritis. "How do you know it ain't something else?" he asks. Because, she tells him, "I had it — had it much worse than you — had it so bad I could only walk on crutches. And now look at me; not a trace of it left — cured — completely." For a few seconds Simon is dubious. Then, with a shiver of excitement running through his body, he asks who the doctor was and whether she thinks the doctor would cure him. The doctor is "Amelia Blazer ... And oh lord, is she a whiz on arthritis," the woman tells Simon. Everything is done by injections — "And oh is she a miracle worker! In three months I put away my crutches and started using canes. In six months I put away my canes. And now look at me!" Simon gets the address of Doctor Balzer, and as he slowly moves from the store into the warm sun he "felt like raising his head to the sky and howling his joy like an animal."

It is not the sheer fact of growing old that disturbs Simon McKeever. He knows that for himself "each stage of life brought its own adventure when a man wasn't dead in his heart." A man had nothing to regret in growing old. What frightens Simon is "the horror of having to lie twisted and helpless in a bed, endlessly, day and night, without function or purpose, while life passed him by. When a man was like that he was nothing, he was ... garbage." It was four years since he had first felt the stiffness in his hips, and two years since he had to quit working because his hands would no longer function properly. The practical problems of getting to Glendale thus seem unimportant to Simon. Four hundred miles from the Finney Home there was a doctor who had a special cure for him, and although it was an enormous distance for a man who was no longer young and had no means, "even ten thousand miles wouldn't count if it meant getting well."

As soon as he returns to the Finney Home from his day's outing, Simon begins to make plans for his journey to Glendale. He seeks the aid of Thomas Finney who, fearful of losing McKeever's pension money, refuses to help and forbids Simon to leave the Home. Undaunted, Simon and some of the other pensioners get together $1.85, two oranges, and a coat. The next day they trick Finney into driving Simon to the main highway, where he gets a bus that takes him across the county line. It is a good beginning, but Simon still has three hundred and seventy-eight miles to go.

Once on the road, Simon's exhilaration begins to give way to tedium. Traffic is slow, and few drivers seem interested in stopping for the shabbily dressed old man. As the cars continue to pass him by, Simon begins to think of the time when, at the age of sixty-one, he had thumbed his way across Arizona into New Mexico; he thinks of the time in 1930 when he was on a refining job outside Los Angeles and construction was shut down in the middle, the men laid off, the pipes and girders left to rust; he thinks of Caroline, the girl he had given a hitch to in 1930, who rode with him throughout the day and into the night with a dead baby in her arms. And as despair begins to set in, Simon thinks of all the hopeful dreams he has had — especially his dream "to fix up a book, a monumental book, that others could read." He would call his book *The Path of Man*. It would be in two parts: "The first section would hold all of the material he had ever read about Man's destiny on earth — provided it was sensible — it would describe the world, and the changing of the world by men, the golden endeavor; and the second part would have selections from Debs and Upton Sinclair and London and Whitman and thinkers like that. This part of the book would tell the role of the forgotten man, it would prove that the common man, as the doer of the world, was not yet understood or rewarded. And it would begin with a quotation from Abraham Lincoln, 'God must love the common man, he made so many of him.' "

Later in the day, and still without a ride, Simon begins to wonder if his dream was not like the baby in Caroline's arms, if he was not a fool to have started in the first place. But Simon refuses to be overcome by despair; he tells himself that he is "an idiot to get so moody," and before long he does get his first hitch. Simon has trouble getting into the car which has stopped for him — it is here that Maltz describes literally the way William Stevenson had gotten into his car — but he finally manages to maneuver himself into the seat, and with sweat dripping down his body murmurs happily, "Ice broken at last."

And so it is, though at times the remainder of the trip to Glendale is to be harrowing. A salesman takes Simon to a bus station where he spends part of the night reading *The Dance of Life* before falling asleep on one of the benches. The next day is better for Simon in terms of mileage, but it is not nearly good enough. By seven o'clock in the evening Simon finds that he is less than eighty miles further along the road to Los Angeles than he had been the previous day. Slowly, painfully, he continues to walk by the roadside until he is so fatigued that he begins to feel lightheaded. He comes to a bridge and remembers that the underside always provides good shelter for a man on the road. He makes his way down a path, hoping that one of the road tramps has left a cooking tin, a stool, or even a good rock bed for a fire. Instead, he finds a half-crazed young hop-head named Harold Malone, who is sitting alongside one of the concrete pillars with a boiling pot of stew in front of him. Simon is curious about the young man whose face has "a brooding quality and a touch of bitter disdain," but he is too hungry to enjoy conversation. Malone senses that Simon wants some of the stew and begins to taunt him: "It's a good stew. Fish I caught today in the Merced River. It's got potatoes in it, celery, onions. But I won't give you any," he tells Simon. "Not on your life. I'll only sell it. You got any money?" Simon offers him his last forty-eight cents but Malone wants more: "It's inflation time," he yells at Simon. "I need a dollar; I got something to buy." When Simon tells him that the forty-eight cents is all he has, Malone erupts angrily, "Damn it, I'm no sucker any more. Nobody makes a fool out of me. I'd rather cut my head off first. I'm through!" Then, sullenly, he says, "Well, all right. You can have forty-eight cents' worth, no more." So saying, he fills a bowl two-thirds full, takes the money from Simon, and "with a thin, cruel and terrible grin of satisfaction, he begins to eat the stew himself." He then kicks over the pot, spilling whatever is left of the stew, takes a knife from his pocket, strokes the blade across his throat, and begins to cry. Minutes later, he picks up his bag and, without a word, disappears into the darkness.

Simon is terrified by his encounter with young Malone, yet it is just because of this encounter that he is finally able to understand the meaning of the nightmare that has plagued him for so long. Earlier, as he sat watching Malone smack his lips maliciously over the stew, Simon began to recall the one event in his life that he had always tried to forget: The time was a summer night in 1921. Simon was then working in San Pedro and had become friends with Paul Simmons, a longshoreman who was a local organizer of the I.W.W. Although he had too many serious differences with the Wobblies to become a member of the I.W.W., Simon would occasionally attend one of the picnics held by the Wobblies in their attempt to raise money. On that Saturday night in 1921, there was a dance and beer party in the I.W.W. hall. Without warning, sixty members of the local Ku Klux Klan burst through the door and began to wreck the hall. When they were finished, they dragged Paul Simmons outside and had him tarred and feathered. That was the night Simon had never been able to forget. And now, after watching and listening to

Malone, and once again recalling the sight of his friend having hot tar poured on him, Simon realizes who the men are who always haunt his dreams by squatting like buzzards around a truck under which his own body lies and calling him "cockroach." Now, he also understands why he is still afraid of them, as he is still afraid of the hop-head. It is not physical fear, but a fear "that his life, as he had lived it and believed in it, was a fraud; a fear that men walked the earth like blind moles to a blind and aimless end. . . ." If men could so easily lose their humanity, then perhaps the world really was a jungle and would never be anything else. Simon "yearned and needed to believe that there was meaning to his life and that there was joy in being a man, even a common anonymous Man, and that Men together were more than beasts in the field."

When he falls asleep later that night, Simon once again has a nightmare — only this one is different. Faces waver before his eyes, speak rapidly, and vanish; a harsh voice tells him that he'll "pass over tonight; this is the last hunger and the last cold; this is the way a life always ends, in garbage and empty motion"; he tries to rise and discovers that during the night someone has fastened iron shackles around his legs; a group of men appear and drag him over the ground as a voice shouts, "Over the cliff with him, he's garbage, he's pissed up the world enough already." Simon then opens his eyes and finds himself in a courtroom; it is he who is on trial, and the charge is that "He's garbage. Why was he ever born?" Simon pleads with his friends to testify for him but they are unable to help: "What's there to testify about in this world?" the figure of a friend asks. "You get born an' you grow old an' you end up like garbage, like the lice that a hard rain shakes off a tree. It's all confused. It's a dream and a mystery to me." No one can testify for Simon, not even his wife, who turns and twists each night in her coffin thinking of the burned and shriveled flesh of their dead daughter. Simon feels stunned and betrayed: "I'm the loneliest man in the world," he thinks in a moment of rare self-pity. But when he gazes upon the people about him and listens to their cries of sorrow, "he saw with utmost clarity that he was no more alone than they." And then "a feeling of exquisite relief entered his heart and he wondered why he had been so long in understanding it. Each man and woman alone and groping in the universe . . . and yet not alone, but striving together. And he knew suddenly that in spite of everything he still heard the music, and he still believed there was a good path to be trod. Strength flowed into his veins.

His body pulsed and shivered and beat. He held out both arms in an agony of rapture and shouted, 'I believe! ... I believe what a man lives for!' "

Events occur rapidly for Simon after the night's dream. When he awakens he is unable to recall the dream itself, yet he knows "there had been a magic in it [for] he felt its balm in his heart." He is eager to continue his trip to Glendale, and begins to climb up the same path he had descended the previous evening. But before he can reach the side of the highway, he passes out: he has had too much sun and too little food. Seconds later a car carrying the Cooley family drives by and one of the children sees Simon lying in the grass.[8] The Cooleys give Simon some milk and crackers, and his strength returns. There is no room in the car for him, but he is grateful for the food. "He was a bit hungry still and a bit disgruntled also, but on the whole he was feeling ... elegant." Soon after the Cooleys leave, a station wagon, driven by an elderly woman with a white-haired man sitting next to her, stops alongside Simon. He finally has his "golden hitch" to Los Angeles.

In the hours that follow, Simon decides that everything has indeed become magical. Not only is he being taken directly to Los Angeles; even more, he is in the company of a remarkable couple, Margaret and Edgar Cochrane. They are pleasantly cordial to Simon, as they are frankly curious about him. By the time the afternoon is over, they know what Simon has done in his life and what he aspires to do. He even tells the Cochranes about his big project — his book, *The Path of Man*. To Simon's amazement, they like the idea: "I'd call it an anthology *about* the common man *for* the common man," Margaret Cochrane suggests. Simon is overwhelmed. He wants to know about the garrulous couple with whom he has been traveling. He learns that they both had been teachers; and, although both of them are now retired, Edgar Cochrane is still a consultant to the Department of Agriculture. Simon wants to know more; he wants to know Cochrane's age. "I'm eighty-two, sonny," the white-haired man tells the delighted McKeever, "I'm one hell of a tough mule." Simon can no longer contain his happiness and bursts out, "Oh Lord, I'm so damn glad you folks picked me up! Aside from the hitch — and that's wonderful — you don't know what it means to be meeting you. Everybody telling me to lay down and throw in the sponge — I knew they were cockeyed. Now I can tell them about you folks."

For the remainder of the ride Simon's enthusiasm is undaunted.

And when the car finally arrives in downtown Los Angeles later that night he insists upon going directly to the home of his "miracle doctor." Although it is late, the Cochranes drive Simon to Glendale, where he manages to see the doctor that very evening. But what she tells him makes him feel "utterly empty inside" for the first time in his life. There is no miracle injection; the woman Simon had met in the drugstore was an hysteric with high blood pressure, not a former arthritic. Simon cannot walk properly, the doctor tells him, because of a bony growth in his hips and knees — a condition known as degenerative arthritis. Nothing can prevent or cure Simon's condition; it's because of the work he did and his age. At best, Simon is told, his condition will stay as it is. On the other hand, it could deteriorate rapidly: there is the possibility, he is warned, that eventually he will not be able to walk at all, that he will end up in a bed, helpless.

Stunned, Simon leaves the doctor's home and returns to Los Angeles, where he sits on a park bench, lost and forlorn, the taste of bile filling his mouth. As the initial shock passes, he understands that he is "really and truly old . . . and [is] prepared to admit it"; in a way it is even satisfying to him to know that his illness is the harvest of his work rather than an accident. What he cannot accept is the vacancy that is now his life: he foresees nothing for himself except "empty hours in a rocking chair." What he needs is something to fill the emptiness, and in a sudden, "tempestuous burst," he realizes that *The Path of Man — his* book — would be a perfect project to fill the void. "If he could only be at work on his book," Simon thinks, "he would be content in a rocking chair, even a bed." Once again Simon is stirred by such a keen optimism and strength that he wonders if he might be possessed by some spirit. He returns to Santabello and the Finney Home, his journey at an end. Simon will die in the boarding home, he knows that; but it is his book, not death, that now concerns him. The world will be a wonderful place someday, Simon thinks to himself as he goes to rejoin his friends; it will take time, and there will be a lot of disappointments before then, a lot of long trips for nothing. But his book will help: it will agitate the minds of men; it will "move the world one inch forward."

IV   *Thought Control*

The reviews of *The Journey of Simon McKeever* were generally very favorable[9] — of all Maltz's work, only *The Cross and the Arrow* received a better press — and the aristocratic, archly conservative Commonwealth Club of California even awarded Maltz its annual silver medal for literary distinction. Yet by the time *Simon McKeever* was published in May, 1949, it already had become something of a minor *cause célèbre* — a symbol of the unrelenting determination of the Hollywood witch hunters to enforce the blacklist against The Hollywood Ten and other "unfriendly" members of the Left.

Shortly before the publication of *Simon McKeever,* Maltz received several copies of the novel from his publisher, Little, Brown. He gave a copy to his film agent, who decided that, the blacklist notwithstanding, she would try to "sell" the novel to one of the major Hollywood studios. (Until that time, the blacklist had applied only to the *employment* of The Hollywood Ten; nothing in the Waldorf Statement mentioned the use of original material.) Within a week after its submission, three companies asked a price for it; and a few days after that the film rights to *The Journey of Simon McKeever* were sold to 20th Century Fox. The Fox Studios immediately put a screenwriter to work on the story, hired Jules Dassin to direct the film, and began negotiations with Walter Huston to play the title role. Maltz, of course, was delighted, and issued a statement to the effect that he regarded the purchase of his novel "as revealing a broadening policy on the part of Hollywood and one that reflected a more intelligent attitude toward the indicted writers."[10] Immediately after the release of this statement, the organization known as The Motion Picture Society for the Preservation of American Ideals (which had provided many of the friendly witnesses for the Hollywood Hearings) began to exert pressure on 20th Century-Fox to cancel their production plans for *Simon McKeever.* On April 12, the Fox Studios released the following statement: "Twentieth Century-Fox Film Corporation announced today that it will not produce the recently acquired property 'The Journey of Simon McKeever,' by Albert Maltz." When asked the reason for the withdrawal, a studio representative would only say, "You have the statement. There is nothing more."[11] And nothing more was said: the film was never produced.[12] The incident, however, did prompt several book reviewers to castigate the film industry. Lewis Gannett, writing in the *New York Herald Tribune,* perhaps most forcefully expressed the reviewers' indignation; he first noted that whatever its weaknesses,

Simon McKeever was an "appealing and heart-warming story of the essential dignity of man in America," and then concluded his review by asking if the Hollywod moguls didn't realize just "how closely their action seems to parallel Communist procedures of thought control in Russia."[13]

V   Some New Writing and Mill Point

Distressing as the action of 20th Century-Fox may have been, Maltz had little time to dwell upon it. A month after the publication of *The Journey of Simon McKeever,* the Court of Appeals upheld the conviction of The Hollywood Ten and Maltz devoted most of the next twelve months to legal conferences and nationwide speaking engagements on behalf of the Ten. Occasionally, perhaps once a month, he would visit William Stevenson, who had become quite deaf and infirm. (When Stevenson finally read *The Journey of Simon McKeever,* he had only two comments: the first was that there were many things in the book that had not really happened; the other was that there were a lot of other things he could tell Maltz about himself if Maltz wanted to write any more stories.[14]) For the most part, however, Maltz devoted whatever free time he had to getting some new writing done.[15]

First, Maltz completed a short story entitled "Circus Come to Town," which was published in the June, 1950, issue of *Masses & Mainstream.*[16] Somewhat reminiscent of the stories he wrote in the 1930s, "Circus Come to Town" tells of the exploitation of a group of young boys by a circus pusher.The boys are too poor to buy tickets to the circus, and can gain admission only by helping to put up the Big Tent and setting up the seats. The work is exhausting, and although the boys finally are allowed in the Big Tent, some quickly fall asleep, while the rest sit with glazed eyes, not knowing what they are watching. Yet, despite the callousness of the circus pusher and his assistant — "What the hell," the assistant says as he looks at the boys asleep in the stands, "we got the matinee on; didn't think we'd make it. Pretty good house, too." — "Circus Come to Town," like *The Journey of Simon McKeever*, is less political than most of Maltz's earlier works; neither the boys nor the pusher seems to exemplify the American condition as much as they do the human condition. "Circus Come to Town" received the Normandy Pen Award for literature in 1952.

While completing "Circus," Maltz read about "several men who had been fired from the Brooklyn Navy Yard for Kafka-esque reasons of a political nature."[17] Intrigued by the accounts in the newspapers, he obtained the transcripts from the attorney involved in the case and began to write what he intended to be a novella based upon this material. But before he got very far into the story, the case of The Hollywood Ten reached its almost inevitable conclusion. On June 28, 1950, Maltz was incarcerated in a Washington jail and shortly thereafter was moved to a federal prison in Mill Point, West Virginia, where he was to remain until his release on April 3, 1951.

CHAPTER 8

A Long Journey

AFTER his release from prison, Maltz went directly to Mexico. It was the time of the Korean War and the McCarthy witch hunts; the House Committee on un-American activities had returned to Hollywood for further investigations, and mass blacklistings had begun in the radio, television, and film industries. Moreover, by Executive Order, passports apparently were being arbitrarily denied to people of left-wing background.[1] However, passports were not needed to go to Mexico, and because he had come out of prison unwell and "needed some emotional surcease from political combat," Maltz settled with his family in Cuernavaca. Almost at once he started to work on the draft of a prison novel, began to dictate some five hundred pages of notes about his experience at Mill Point, and wrote an article for *Masses & Mainstream* on "The Whiskey Men" — those inmates of the prison at Mill Point, who had been found "guilty of the crime of distilling illicit liquor or of transporting it, of selling or drinking it." (These men, who comprised about sixty percent of the prison inmates, turned to illegal whiskey making for both cultural and economic reasons: "Left to their own devices by an indifferent government," Maltz wrote, "faced by a forbidding outside world and a submarginal existence in their home community, they turn to whiskey making.... Actually a type of malformed social rebellion is present here, and the social cost of it is immense.")[2]

At about the same time that he was writing "The Whiskey Men," Maltz "got the notion of going back to the materials about the Brooklyn Navy Yard and doing them as a long one-act play."[3] The result was "The Morrison Case," a play about a man named Peter Morrison who is dismissed from his job at the Brooklyn Navy Yard

118

after a loyalty hearing board decides that he *must* be a member of the Communist Party. The essence of the drama is summed up in Morrison's final statement to the Board:

I'm saying that this whole business is rotten from the beginning, it's rotten fish. It doesn't make no difference I'm not a Communist. I think your job is to get rid of anybody who thinks different from you do — and that ain't American, it's Hitler Germany, that's what it is! I read a newspaper you don't like — that's it! I ain't fighting for my job now. My job's gone. I got no more chance than a mouse in a trap. I think my job was gone the minute I was charged, before I walked in here. And the worst of it is — when I go home and see my wife and kids, I'll know I could've saved my job. I'll say baby, I'm out, I'm blacklisted. I'll say we're gonna lose this house of ours, baby, and we're against some awful hard times. But I could've saved it all — you know how? By joining the Ku Klux Klan ten years ago! And you know what she'll say to me? Just what I'm saying to you right now! If that's what the job means, they can take the job and shove it!

When "The Morrison Case" was completed, Maltz tried to find a producer for it; he discovered, not totally unexpectedly, that suddenly there was no market for his play anywhere in the United States. Eventually, "The Morrison Case" was produced and published in several Eastern European countries, but it still remains unavailable in the United States.

I *Handwritten Notes*

Both "The Morrison Case" and "The Whiskey Men" were incidental to Maltz's main project at this time, the writing of *A Long Day in a Short Life*. The idea for the book came shortly after Maltz was imprisoned in the Washington jail: "Naturally," Maltz recalled some years ago, "I had been automatically absorbing every possible detail about jail life and the other inmates during my days there from the first moment of entrance. However, once I got the idea for the novel, I proceeded to make extensive notes for it — particularly data on the men I met, the prison routines, the food, dialogue ... everything that any writer does in a 'research' situation. I imagine that I accumulated about forty or more pages of handwritten notes."[4]

Pencil and paper were easily obtainable, and since he was locked in his cell twenty-one out of every twenty-four hours, Maltz had more than enough time to jot down his notes. But there was a serious problem as to what he was to do with the notes once they were on paper. Prison regulations forbade him from taking the notes with him when he was transferred to the federal prison; consequently, Maltz decided to spend his idle hours memorizing the forty-odd pages of notes. And as soon as he arrived at the prison camp in West Virginia, he once again put the notes on paper. Before leaving Mill Point, Maltz followed the same procedure: the notes were committed to memory and then destroyed. Thus by the time he got to Cuernavaca, Maltz not only had managed to work out the broad idea for his new work, but he also had specific notes on individuals in the Washington jail whom he intended to use as the basis of characters in *A Long Day*. The first draft of the novel was quickly completed, and by the early part of 1954 Maltz was ready to send *A Long Day in a Short Life* to a publisher.[5]

II   A Long Day in a Short Life

In its tone and structure, *A Long Day in a Short Life* is reminiscent of Maltz's novella, "Season of Celebration." The events in both works occur within a twenty-four-hour period, and both stories are concerned with men who have been imprisoned: in "Season of Celebration" the prison is the Bowery flophouse and in *A Long Day in a Short Life* it is the District Jail in Washington, D.C. In "Season of Celebration," it is economic injustice which makes prisoners of the inhabitants of the Hotel Raleigh; in *A Long Day,* it is judicial harshness and racial discrimination. In "Season of Celebration" the story centers on Jimmy O'Shaughnessy and Harold Blessy; in *A Long Day in a Short Life* the focus of interest is on Floyd Varney and Huey Wilson.

Unlike O'Shaughnessy and Blessy, however, Floyd Varney and Huey Wilson never meet; they have been imprisoned for different reasons and their cells are on different tiers. Varney, a white man, has been charged with second-degree murder and is awaiting sentence; his story dominates the first half of the novel. Wilson, a young Negro, has been charged with felonious assault with a dangerous weapon and is awaiting a preliminary hearing; his story dominates the second half of *A Long Day in a Short Life*.

Varney has killed a man: about that there is no question. What is at issue is whether the killing was premeditated. The events, in outline, are simple: after work one evening, Varney had stopped for a cocktail at a local bar where he met "a handsome woman in her late twenties who was destined to shatter his life." Harriet Peterson was the wife of a textile manufacturer and the mother of a young daughter. To revenge herself for her husband's adulterous affairs, she recently had sought to have affairs of her own. Floyd Varney became her pickup on that evening. Two days later, the affair was continued, only this time they were interrupted by Mrs. Peterson's husband. A struggle ensued between the two men, and when Peterson reached for a knife, Varney struck him across the larynx with the outer edge of his open hand. The blow fractured the Adam's apple and caused a hemorrhage into Peterson's windpipe. Within a few minutes he was dead of suffocation.

Varney, assuming that Peterson was merely stunned, fled from the room, leaving behind his hat and coat. The police arrived shortly after, and by that time Mrs. Peterson "had fabricated a version of the events that was designed to protect her honor before society." She told the police that Varney had raped her: "she bore no ill-will toward Varney, and had no desire to do him harm. The lies she impulsively told concerned an utter stranger, who had used force upon a chaste wife and mother." But in so doing she overlooked the fact that Varney's initialed overcoat and hat were still in the room. The next day Floyd Varney was arrested and soon after was indicted for homicide.

Varney, by nature a lonely and distrustful man, is unable to understand what has happened to him:

He had worked like a dog from the time he was ten, but what sort of control had he had over his own fortunes? So very little — always on the outside looking in! Other men held down steady jobs during an economic depression, but he was one of those who got the rough end of the stick — nothing open, buddy. War came and other men got through it all right, but hard-luck Varney ended in a hospital. How many men were there who went to bed with other men's wives, and had themselves a bit of fun, and nothing ever came of it? Not Varney! It was his luck to meet up with a crazy husband, and a lying bitch of a wife, and a thick-headed jury that couldn't understand that the killing was an accident. All of his life it had been the same — but why — how — for what reason?[6]

Whatever the reason — accident, fate, his own distrustful nature — it becomes unimportant in terms of the sentence imposed upon him. For Maltz, like Theodore Dreiser in *An American Tragedy,* is as concerned with the inability of the judicial system to respond adequately to certain crimes as he is with the forces leading to the crime. "There are decisions," Dreiser told a reporter shortly after the publication of *An American Tragedy,* "which casually chosen juries of men, unused to judge human motives and actions, are ludicrously unfit to render."[7] However guilty Clyde Griffiths may be, and whatever he may be guilty of, he is no more guilty, Dreiser argues in *An American Tragedy,* than the jury that convicts him. And however culpable Floyd Varney may be, he is less guilty than the judge who sentences him to a federal penitentiary for a term of from twenty-five years to life:

> Like many occupants of the bench [Maltz wrote], Judge Stokey was un-fitted for his job. This was not because he was a stupid or a vicious man, since he was neither. In ordinary day to day contact he was decent and reasonably tolerant. Nevertheless, the position of a Judge is one of extra-ordinary responsibility; the power to send men to prison is an awesome one that, by any profound standards, calls for deep human wisdom, for social insight, and for unusual objectivity. Of these qualities Judge Stokey possessed no greater measure than was to be expected from one who had achieved his position by virtue of a conventional history; from Harvard law school to the Washington firm of his uncle; next, to a position on the legal staff of the Department of Justice; following that, an appointment as an Assistant Federal Attorney; and finally, after ten years of being a prosecutor, of associating with the right people in the right circles, and of supporting the political party in power, he had received an appointment to the Federal Bench. As a result, it could not be said that his lively intelli-gence had a more profound grasp of the problems of crime and penology than that of many another citizen. Indeed, somewhat less, since he had had ten years of conditioning in the mentality of a prosecutor.[8]

Judge Stokey is simply incapable of passing judgment fairly. As he draws his black robe about him after passing sentence on Varney he is clearly a figure of death, not a minister of justice. And at first Varney's response to the sentence is nothing more than "an involuntary howl, as of a dog struck brutally without warning." But later that day, as the impact of the sentence becomes clear to him, and his determination increases to deny to Judge Stokey the satisfaction of his long imprisonment, Floyd Varney commits suicide.

Huey Wilson is of a stronger and more determined nature than Floyd Varney. His imprisonment, unlike that of Varney, is totally without justification. For Huey Wilson is guilty of nothing more than being black. He is attacked by four white youths after he has taken part in a demonstration against segregation in the city high schools, and he and Art Ballou, the leader of the white youths, are arrested on suspicion of disorderly conduct. The next morning the charge against Wilson suddenly becomes intoxication, resisting arrest, and felonious assault with deadly weapons; the charge against Ballou remains disorderly conduct. The police clearly are out to "get" the young black. "They're out to frame you good," he is told. "You know that knife this fellow Ballou had? Well, that's disappeared already, none of the cops ever seen it. It seems that feller you sent to the hospital has an old man who's got some pull with the police. That detective said they was gon t'send you up for five years."

But it is not just Huey Wilson whom the police are going to set up; they are also working up false charges against Thomas McPeak, a white Southerner. McPeak, a machinist in a Ford plant in Detroit, has come to Washington for the wedding of his niece and has been in the city less than an hour when he sees Ballou and his friends attacking Huey Wilson. Instinctively, McPeak pulls Ballou off Wilson, and for the next couple of minutes the fifty-year-old Georgia cracker and the eighteen-year-old black high school student battle the white youths. When the police finally arrive, McPeak is arrested together with Wilson and Ballou, and he too is charged on suspicion of disorderly conduct. And, like Wilson, he learns the next day that the charge against him has been changed to intoxication, resisting arrest, and felonious assault with a deadly weapon.

The police, however, are not really interested in McPeak. Although they cannot understand how a white Southerner could possibly make common cause with a Black, they do not really want to "get" him. If anything, they want to get rid of him, since he is the only one who can offer evidence on Wilson's behalf. "They're working up false charges on both of us," McPeak tells Wilson. "But you're the one they're out to git." The police want McPeak to leave town; "They don't want me testifying. Said they'd let me go free if I took the first bus home." Huey wants to know what McPeak intends to do, but the older man only replies, "Shucks, how the hell do I know? I don't know where I stand any more'n you do. I came all the way from Detroit t'go to my niece's weddin, and now look where I am. I wasn't wantin any trouble."

As the hours go by — time spent behind bars and, when possible, in conversation with the other inmates — McPeak begins to reach a decision about where he stands. Slowly but inexorably he begins to turn away from Huey Wilson. He just does not want to risk imprisonment: "He had his conscience, and his sense of solidarity, and his sense of shame, but they were withering away in this cage of steel and wire and stone." He had done enough; it had not been his fight in the first place. This was not like a union struggle where he would stick to the end no matter what happened. This "was a matter of race prejudice, it was as old as the United States itself, and it wouldn't be solved in a day." There was no reason for Tom McPeak to go to jail over it.

Still, McPeak cannot forget about Huey Wilson. Not only is he constantly reminded of the youth's plight by the hatred which the white inmates have for the black prisoners; he is increasingly impressed with Huey's pride and determination. In the few hours that he has been in the district jail, Huey Wilson has become the focal point of the racial bias in the prison. And before long a series of minor incidents culminates in an open confrontation between Art Ballou, Huey, and the System.

Huey has been assigned to the mess detail, and is serving second helpings at the noon-time meal when he hears a voice call to him, "Hey, boy, beans here ... Here boy." Huey tries to ignore the taunt, but Ballou signals the guard and indignantly informs him: "I want some beans, but that damn coon passed me by! He damn well heard me, too!" "He called me 'boy,' " Huey tells the guard. "I don't pay attention to anyone calls me that. I'm not a boy, I'm a man; and I'm sure not *his* 'boy.' " The guard orders one of the other men to serve Ballou and the incident seems to be over. But minutes later, as Huey is making his way down an aisle with a bowl of beets, he once again hears Ballou's voice, "Beets here, boy. Very light." This time the guard orders Huey to serve Ballou but Huey refuses: "I told you before, I'm not his 'boy'. I won't serve anybody calls me that." At this point the issue suddenly changes; it is no longer a feud between two inmates but a matter of obedience to the authority of the guard. "I gave you an order to serve that man," the guard says to Huey. "You do it, or I'll write you up for discipline." Huey slowly moves to Ballou and asks, "How you want it?" Ballou, grinning, replies, "Very light ... you f— nigger." Huey then takes the bowl, still a third filled with pickled beets and onions, and flings it into Ballou's face. There is a brief scuffle, and both youths are given four days in solitary confinement.

The immediate impact of this encounter upon McPeak is to make his decision more difficult: "Somehow everything had been made worse for him by the dinner fight, and by the fact that Huey was due for punishment." And the decision is made even more difficult when, during the evening meal, the mess men announce that they refuse to do any more serving. "I won't serve anybody who insults me," one of the men tells the guard. "He called me 'boy'. It happens I'm a man." The guard orders the men back to work, but they refuse to move: "You like as well know we've done all of us quit ... We're on strike." When the guard threatens to put all the mess men on report, McPeak indignantly yells at the guard, "If that ain't the most Goddamn unfairest thing I ever seen, I don't know what is ... you're writin up the wrong guys. They didn't start this ... you're discriminaten agin those men."

McPeak is immediately sent back to his cell. No sooner does the door close, however, than it opens again and McPeak hears his name called by the tier guard. As he follows a guard into a small office he fully expects to be disciplined for his outburst. Instead, he is confronted by Detective Stoner, who has his suitcase and a bus ticket for Detroit. "There's a bus leavin for Detroit in about an hour," Stoner tells him. "A pal of mine on the Detroit force will be waitin for you. You pull in there like you should and all charges here'll be dropped. There won't even be an arrest mark on you." But McPeak doesn't like the idea. "I don't like bein pushed around," he tells Stoner. "I come here for a family git-together and a weddin, and I aim t'go to it." Stoner angrily warns McPeak that unless he is out of town when "that nigger" goes up for his hearing, "You'll pull time, Mister, an I mean time. We'll show you what pushing can be." Of all the things Stoner might have said to McPeak, this was the least well calculated. For, contrary to its intended effect, what Stoner says inflames that area of McPeak's feelings that is most explosive — "his resentment of arbitrary authority." And so, with his face red with anger, his eyes blazing, and his chunky figure set as though for a fight, Tom McPeak finally makes his stand: "So show me!" he yells at Stoner. "An I'll show you a thing or two, I will! I'm goin into that Hearin and I'm gone speak the truth. I'm gone testify for the colored boy and I'm gone tell evry last part of this lousy frame-up you're tryin to pull. When I git through talkin, God damn it, it ain't me who'll pull time, it'll be you...."

McPeak has made his point, and so has Maltz. The System has destroyed Floyd Varney, but it will not destroy Huey Wilson *or*

Thomas McPeak. Varney had no way of fighting the injustice of the System represented by Judge Stokey: years in prison or suicide are the alternatives he sees available to him. Huey Wilson, on the other hand, who is arrested because he is black, and is sent to the Hole because he refuses to serve anyone who calls him "boy" or "nigger," has learned that he can survive both the system and the Hole because what he wants above all else is "to be what his father called a real man." And Tom McPeak has come to realize that the principle of trade union solidarity is as potent a force against authority in federal prison as it is in a Ford plant. From the moment McPeak had pinned a union button on his shirt he had understood that even as an anonymous laboring man he was stronger than himself because he was not alone, that he had the power to say "We strike." It is this sense of solidarity that makes the Georgia cracker stir with pride when a group of strange, black mess men, stick together in the face of authority, and that finally makes it impossible for him to desert young Huey Wilson.

III   Tough and Tender

When *A Long Day in a Short Life* was completed in the early part of 1954, Maltz sent the manuscript to Little, Brown and Company, the publisher of his three previous novels. Little, Brown inexplicably turned it down, as did eighteen other publishing houses. (At the same time, Maltz received contracts for the work from sixteen foreign companies.) The novel eventually was given to International Publishers, who brought out *A Long Day* in 1957.

However, the publication of *A Long Day in a Short Life* by International Publishers, the left-wing house which in 1937 had published *The Way Things Are,* virtually guaranteed that the novel would be scantily reveiwed. It *was* discussed in *Afro-American* by Saunders Redding, who wrote that "*A Long Day in a Short Life* is both tough and tender. Its toughness derives from its truth; its tenderness derives from the author's deep compassion."[9] And the *Pittsburgh Courier* carried a brief review under the heading, "One of the 'Hollywood Ten' Speaks": "While drawing a clear and shameful picture of racial conditions in our nation's capital early in this decade [wrote Marjorie Jackson], Maltz tells an engrossing story with a minimum of propagandizing, and fills his book with sharply delineated portraits of society's misfits and how they got that way."[10] There were also brief reviews in the *Daily Worker,* the

National Guardian, and the *Times Literary Supplement.* But that was about all. *A Long Day in a Short Life* did not receive a single review in the regular commercial press.

IV *Another Blacklist*

Part of the reticence of Little, Brown and the other publishing houses to handle Maltz's novel almost certainly can be traced to five confidential directives issued by the State Department between February and June, 1953. They resulted in the removal of several hundred books by some forty authors from the libraries of the United States Information Service abroad. The March directive, as reported in the International Edition of the *New York Times,* stated that the works of "all Communist authors, any publication continually publishing Communist propaganda and questionable material lending undue emphasis to Communist personalities and their statements," should be banned from all public libraries and information centers of the United States Information Service.[11] The directive added that "for the purposes of this instruction, authors who obviously follow the Communist line or participate in Communist front organizations will be considered Communists and their works banned."

Another directive specifically named sixteen writers whose works were to be banned from libraries abroad, regardless of the subject matter of the work. (The sixteen were James A. Allen, Herbert Aptheker, Millen Brand, Earl Browder, Howard Fast, Philip S. Foner, Helen Goldfrank, William Gropper, Dashiell Hammett, Donald Henderson, Julius Hlavaty, William M. Mandel, Lawrence K. Rosinger, Morris U. Schappes, Bernhard J. Stern, and Gene Weltfish.) Most of these writers were included in the State Department directive which called for the removal of works by authors who had cited the Fifth Amendment to avoid telling Congressional groups about their political affiliations. Because Maltz had cited the First rather than the Fifth Amendment during the Hollywood Hearings, he was not listed among the writers whose works were to be removed from libraries in their entirety. But he was not to be ignored: *The Cross and the Arrow,* the least propagandistic of all his novels, was among the books "removed from one or more libraries of the United States Information Service abroad...."[12]

Although the State Department's directives applied only to libraries abroad, librarians in the United States began to remove books by the forty authors from their shelves. As a consequence, these writers became commercial liabilities. Maltz could no more get a novel published by one of the major houses than he could get a Hollywood studio to produce one of his scripts. The blacklist proved to be most effective, and for a while Maltz was indeed an exile in Mexico. Yet even there he was not free from the venom of the McCarthy witch hunters. Shortly after he arrived in Cuernavaca, for example, Maltz read a front-page story in *Excelsior,* the leading newspaper in Mexico, which stated that Gordon Kahn (the author of *The Hollywood Ten*) was founding an American Communist colony in Cuernavaca. The article was based on one which had appeared in the *New York Herald Tribune* under the by-line of the editor, Ogden Reid, and quoted Reid as asserting that Kahn had established a new Hollywood in Cuernavaca in order to give asylum to Communists and their fellow travelers who had lost their ability to function in the studios of Hollywood. Maltz was mentioned as being one of the colleagues whom Kahn had "transported" to Mexico. And three years later, *U.S. News and World Report* announced that "Mexico and Cuba now have become the links in an 'underground railroad' that carries Communist sympathizers from the U.S. to Mexico." A speech by Representative Walter, Chairman of the House Committee on Un-American Activities which listed members of the "Communist colony" in Mexico, was then quoted; Maltz, of course, was included in the list.[13]

Despite the blacklist, as well as pressure from the press and Congressional committees, Maltz continued to write. Like many of the Hollywood outcasts, he became part of what has been called "the Hollywood Underground."[14] Murray Schumach, in his book on movie and television censorship, *The Face on the Cutting Room Floor,* describes the way in which the blacklisted managed to get work:

First there is the use of the 'front.' A blacklisted writer does a script. He knows it will not be produced with his name on it. He approaches a 'clean writer' — one who is not on the blacklist — and suggests that the latter's name be used on the script. For this the front usually gets a fee, sometimes running as high as 50 per cent of the sale price. The front generally does nothing more than lend his name to the script. There are some non-blacklisted writers who have refused to accept payment for this service, an admittedly risky undertaking in the timorous environment of Hollywood. Then there are fronts who do some of the writing with the blacklisted writer. If the blacklisted writer has a reputation, his agent may book the fronts for him.

The producer nearly always knows who the real writer is and often discusses rewrites with him in person. Sometimes stars, whose parts need changing, confer with the blacklisted writer. In the vast majority of cases, the studio that finances and releases the movie knows the identity of the writer behind the front. Nevertheless, a studio maintains over and over again the pretense that it is ignorant of the real writer. This requires a special kind of lógic. The studio, since it claims there is no blacklist, cannot admit it is refusing to use certain writers. That would be an admission that there is a blacklist. At the same time it dare not admit it is using writers who are on the 'nonexistent' blacklist. That would antagonize powerful groups.[15]

Of course, many people on the blacklist could not work at all. There was no way for an actor or director to use a front or pseudonym, nor could those people who had functioned in the studios as readers, secretaries, and electricians. Moreover, those blacklisted writers who did succeed in obtaining work in the manner described by Schumach frequently had to settle for a fraction of the previous fees; Dalton Trumbo, for example, who in 1947 had been under contract to Metro-Goldwyn-Mayer for $75,000 per year to write two films a year, was compelled to write entire scripts for $1,500 to $3,000. But unlike many blacklistees who were forced into other fields of work in order to make a living, many of the writers were at least able to support themselves by means of their craft. And, ironically, some of the most successful films of the 1950s were written by blacklisted writers. Trumbo wrote the script for *The Brave One;* Michael Wilson collaborated on *Bridge on the River Kwai;* Nedrick Young and Hal Smith co-authored *The Defiant Ones;* and Maltz was largely responsible for the script of *The Robe,* one of the most lucrative films in the history of Twentieth-Century Fox. None of these writers, however, were given screen credit for their work; nor could Trumbo, Young, and Smith acknowledge their contributions when the scripts for *The Brave One* and *The Defiant Ones* received Academy Awards. (Young and Smith did receive their awards — in person — but they did so under their pseudonyms.)[16]

V   *The Patriotism of Frank Sinatra*

The first major breakthrough against the blacklist occurred in 1960 when Otto Preminger announced that Dalton Trumbo had written the screenplay of Leon Uris' *Exodus,* which he would produce, and Stanley Kramer retained Nedrick Young to write the scenario for *Inherit the Wind.* Yet, later that same year, Maltz became involved in an incident that demonstrated just how powerful the forces of the American Legion and the Hearst press were in perpetuating the blacklist.

On March 21, Frank Sinatra, then at the peak of his power as a movie star, and "in many ways the most courageous man in Hollywood,"[17] announced that he had hired Maltz to write the script for the film of William Bradford Huie's *The Execution of Private Slovik* (the story of the only American soldier to be executed for desertion since the Civil War). The response from both the Hearst press and the American Legion was immediate and angry. *The New York Journal American* quoted Senator Karl Mundt as saying, "In these uneasy times it is hard to understand that people will grant new opportunities for the injection of communist propaganda into motion picture fare," and itself editorialized that "By hiring him [Maltz], Mr. Sinatra, however much he may delude himself to the contrary, has not struck a blow FOR freedom of expression. He has struck a blow AGAINST efforts of the industry to prevent enemies of our country from using the powerful medium of the movies for an insidiously slanted Communist line."[18] Pressure was brought on disc jockeys not to play Sinatra's records, and the American Legion, Catholic War Veterans, and Amvets warned that they would boycott the film if Maltz were not dismissed. On March 25, the Hearst press addressed itself directly to Sinatra: "In hiring Maltz [the editorial intoned] you are not giving employment to a poor sheep who lost his way but to a real Communist pro.... Therefore, we suggest you consider the request of National Commander Raymond O'Leary of the Catholic War Veterans. Dump Maltz and get yourself a true American writer."[19]

At first, Sinatra defended his hiring of Maltz on the grounds that he had spoken to many screenwriters, "but that it was not until I talked to Albert Maltz that I found a writer who saw the screenplay in exactly the terms I wanted. This is, the Army was right." At the same time, he denounced the attacks "from certain quarters" of those who were trying to connect then-Senator John F. Kennedy, whom Sinatra was actively supporting for the Presidency, with his decision to hire Maltz: "I make movies," Sinatra said. "I do not ask the advice of Senator Kennedy on whom I shall hire. Senator Kennedy does not ask me how he shall vote in the Senate." Sinatra ended his statement on the hiring of Maltz (which was published in *The Hollywood Reporter*) by declaring: "I am prepared to stand on my principles and to await the verdict of the American people when they see 'The Execution of Private Slovik.' I repeat: In my role as a picture-maker, I have — in my opinion — hired the best man to do the job.''[20]

Only occasionally was a voice heard in support of Sinatra: while the Hearst people continued their onslaught, even the Premingers and Kramers remained silent.[21] Finally, on April 8, without first notifying Maltz, Sinatra announced to the press that he was discharging "the best man for the job":

> In view of the reaction of my family, my friends and the American public, I have instructed my attorneys to make a settlement with Albert Maltz and to inform him he will not write the screenplay for "The Execution of Private Slovik."
>
> I had thought the major consideration was whether or not the resulting script would be in the best interests of the United States.
>
> Since my conversations with Mr. Maltz had indicated that he had an affirmative, pro-American approach to the story, and since I felt fully capable as producer of enforcing such standards, I have defended my hiring of Mr. Maltz.
>
> But the American public has indicated it feels the morality of hiring Albert Maltz is the more crucial matter, and I will accept this majority opinion.[22]

Shortly after, Sinatra sold his film rights to *The Execution of Private Slovik*. To this date he has not seen Maltz again, and *Private Slovik* still has not been made into a movie.

VI *The Career of Julian Silva*

As a result of the Sinatra-Slovik affair, Maltz became convinced that he would have to use a pseudonym if he was to have any more stories published in the United States. Actually, the idea of adopting a pseudonym had come up shortly after his release from prison. The blacklist was then at its peak; Maltz had stopped receiving requests to reprint his stories (prior to the blacklist, "Man on the Road" had been widely anthologized), and there clearly was no possibility of any of his stories being purchased for television dramatization. For a while, therefore, he considered using a pseudonym on *A Long Day in a Short Life*. He discussed the matter with his family and friends, some of whom convinced him that to use a pseudonym was to bow to the blacklist; all blacklisted authors, he came to agree, had an obligation to fight for their names.[23] But, "after Sinatra hired and fired me in so public a way [Maltz wrote in 1969], I felt I was more profoundly blacklisted than ever before and that my work could not possibly get a fair shake in the literary market place. So I said the hell with it. I decided to begin over again as a new writer."[24]

Under the name of Julian Silva, Maltz began to submit a number of short stories to various journals. Some of the stories — "Pani" and "Husband and Wife," for example — could not be placed and were eventually published in Europe.[25] On the other hand, "With Laughter," a story about a young pregnant black woman who is refused admittance to a white hospital and must give birth on the street, was sold to *Southwest Review* and some months later won an award as the best short story published in the magazine during 1960–1961.[26] Not long after, an unpublished story was sold to television,[27] and Maltz seemed to have the beginnings of a "new" writing career.

Then, almost unbelievably, Maltz's agent discovered that there was an actual Julian Silva who was submitting manuscripts to the publishing houses. And that was the end of Maltz's career as Julian Silva. His agent decided to send the manuscript of a recently completed novel to England rather than establish a new pseudonym; and in 1967 *A Tale of One January* was published under Maltz's own name by Calder and Boyers.

VII   A Tale of One January

Seven years earlier, while he was still living in Mexico, Maltz met a Frenchwoman, Dounia Wasserstrom, who had been a political prisoner in Auschwitz. Mrs. Wasserstrom had arrived at that most-feared of all concentration camps on a French transport in 1942, and because of her linguistic facility was put to work as an interpreter for the S.S. Three years later, on January 18, 1945, as the Russian armies were approaching the camp, all the remaining prisoners were marched out under guard for an unknown destination. During the first day of the march Mrs. Wasserstrom and a close friend, Janie, managed to escape. When, in 1960, Mrs. Wasserstrom came to know Maltz well, she gave him a detailed account of both the escape and the events subsequent to it. The talks which Maltz had with Dounia Wasserstrom served as the basis for *A Tale of One January.*[28]

Maltz's novel closely follows Mrs. Wasserstrom's account. As such, Auschwitz itself remains in the background: it is the escape rather than the camp which dominates *A Tale of One January.* In fact, when the novel begins, the prisoners — including Claire and Lini, the fictional counterparts of Dounia Wasserstrom and her friend Janie — have already left Auschwitz. They have been forced to march fourteen miles in six hours in the snow before being herded into a barn for a rest. It is at this point that the novel opens with a brief paragraph that foreshadows the escape:

At five in the morning on Claire's twenty-sixth birthday she was embraced by her friend Lini, who gave her a hard-bought gift: two sweet biscuits and a pair of shoes. Claire, knowing their price, wept. Now, some hours later, she was eating the biscuits while she gazed with intense foreboding at the shoes. It was imperative that she take them off her feet, but she was terrified of doing so.

Claire's feet have become frostbitten, and she realizes that it will be impossible for her to continue the march. She wakes Lini, who had fallen asleep as soon as she entered the barn, and tells her that she intends to hide in one of the haystacks (which descend more than seven feet below ground level). Lini is frightened; but she and Claire have been together so long — first in Drancy, the camp outside Paris, then in Birkenau and Auschwitz — that, whatever the danger, she insists upon remaining with her friend. So, as Lini will have it, they burrow their way as far into the hay as they can go, and it is not long before they hear the guards warn the prisoners, "If any of you bitches have hidden in the hay, nothing will happen to you if you come out right now. If we find you hiding, we'll shoot you!" Then there is silence. The last thing Claire and Lini hear before they fall asleep is a rifle shot in the distance.

Almost forty-eight hours later the two women are awakened by the sound of another column of prisoners entering the barn. They huddle together, certain that they will be discovered. And their fears seem to be all-too-justified when the head of a man abruptly pushes through the hay into their hole. But as the man stares at them in disbelief, and Lini muffles a cry, there is a sudden moment of recognition: "In the faint light the women could see that the man's head, so close to them, was shaven, and he could see their kerchiefs." As soon as she is able to speak, Lini asks the man to hide somewhere else. Nodding, he starts to crawl away, stops to tell them not to worry, that "we're the last transport," starts away again, stops once more to inform the women that "I organized a bottle of cognac," and finally disappears.

For what seems like an interminable period, the women are engulfed by a strained silence. Suddenly, there is the sound of dogs barking, the commotion of men moving about, a steady rustling and crunching of hay, the shrill bleat of whistles outside the barn, and the tramping of thousands of feet on the frosty snow. Then, silence once again. The transport has left; but Claire and Lini remain petrified, waiting for a signal from the man who had "organized a bottle of cognac." There is no word, no sound. Twenty minutes go by before they hear a voice call to them. "All right, girls, a bayonet just missed me, but here I am — ha, ha! Coast is clear, come out and have some cognac."

When the women make their way out of the hay they are astonished to see not one but four men. In addition to Otto (the man with the cognac) who is Austrian, there is Norbert, a German, Jurek, a Pole, and Andrey, a Russian. All but Andrey had obviously had modestly favorable jobs in the camp: "They were under-weight, but not cadaverously so, and they were wearing warm civilian clothes rather than the striped ersatz of most prisoners. Both facts meant that they had been in a position to organize some food and clothes in the camp black market." Andrey, on the other hand, is dressed in prison stripes (as are Claire and Lini). And with the exception of Lini, all had been non-Jewish political prisoners.

The first decision the group must make is how they "want to manage — separate or together." There is no disagreement: they will stay together. But there is nothing to eat and they must remain in hiding until the Russians come; somehow they must "manage" that too. Jurek, the youngest member of the group, partially resolves the problems by getting food and some clothing from the farmer in whose barn they are hiding. And later that day, following the farmer's directions, they slip out of the barn and slowly make their way to an empty factory. As they walk through the moonlit snow, Claire is almost overwhelmed by the beauty of the night, and whispers to Lini, "It's so peaceful here, so peaceful ... These few minutes without guards and dogs are worth so much to me that if I had to die now, I don't care." And despite the intense cold which racks their bodies, all are aware of the strong yet bitter bond that has already developed among them, a bond borne of their years in

Auschwitz where "their spirits had learned accommodation to much more than cold — to incessant hunger and unending fear, to the horrible stench of human bodies burning in crematoria, and to all the abuse to which a human being can be subjected and still survive."

Once inside the factory, life begins to return to all the "Mussulmen" from Auschwitz. Apprehensive as they are, they become feverish with excitement and hope. For the first time in years they are able to regard themselves as men and women; for the first time since they were imprisoned they have something other than the crematoria to which they can look forward. For a while, as Jurek once again goes in search of food and clothing, they sit quietly, "thinking of home, of faces, of streets — and wondering if home, faces, streets, still were there." Then they begin to talk: of their lives before the war, of the camps they had been in, of the future that is now a possibility. At first they speak somewhat reluctantly, but as their sense of freedom becomes more secure, as they realize that they are no longer "numbers — slaves — dirt," they talk with an increasing excitement that continues for almost three days. Otto finally brings a halt to the talk; and, not incidentally, causes an irreparable break in the group.

Lini is the first to sense the change in the relationship between the two women and the men. She is beginning to feel like a woman again, and confides to Claire that she is "starved to have a man I like put his arms around me." There is an electricity in the air, Lini tells her friend, and the men will not wait much longer before they ask the women to make love with them. She is quite right. Two days later, Norbert, a quiet, strong man who has survived twelve years in the camps, asks Lini to become his lover. It is Norbert for whom she has been waiting, and with a nod of her head the two go off to a separate room.

But as Claire has foreseen, the situation now becomes precarious for the rest of the group; "now sexuality was vibrant in the room, and they no longer were a family." Now, there is Claire and three men. Jurek, the young Pole, is no problem, for as he tells his friends, "Zosia [the farmer's] sister, is very nice woman. She is not too old for me." Neither Andrey nor Otto, however, has such an outlet, and their passion focuses on Claire. But from the very beginning, Claire has found Otto less likeable than the other men, while Andrey's love of music and his attentive concern for her frostbitten foot has attracted Claire. Yet, despite her affection for

Andrey, she not only tries to soothe Otto's frustration and jealousy but refuses to allow Andrey to consummate his love for her.

For, unlike Lini, Claire is not yet ready for a man: "A man would be too much for me right now," she tells Lini. "I haven't come that far back to life. I just want to eat and sleep and feel happy we're free. . . ." As much as she wants to feel passion again, and as much as she thinks of her freedom, Claire is still a Mussulman bound by the experience of Auschwitz. She cannot forget the sickness or the decay or the maddening manner in which she learned of her husband's extermination; and, above all, she cannot forget about the "child and the apple":

In September [Claire tells Andrey] a transport came to our section. No transport ever came before. Why did this one? I don't know. Seventy-two Jewish children from five to twelve. I saw the document, they'd been hidden by Polish families. Now the Gestapo had them down for the ovens in Birkenau. I watched them from the window. My heart was like a crazy hammer. So innocent and beautiful. There was a conference in my office and I was sent outside. I couldn't speak to them, there were SS and dogs. One boy had a big, red apple. About six years old, nicely dressed, brown hair, brown eyes, so pretty and sweet. He was playing with the apple, rolling it, running after it. The Gestapos came out. They shook hands. All of them went away except one from my office, Kress. He stood looking at the boy. He walked towards him. He called out in Polish. The little lad turned around. Kress bent over — he took hold of his ankles and swung him — and smashed his brains out against a wall. . . . But don't think that was all! He put the apple in his pocket. And that afternoon his wife and child came to visit him. He took the boy on his lap — kissed him — and then he said, 'I have something for you' — and he reached into the desk drawer and gave him the apple.

To Claire, the death of the young boy has become the death of all children: "It ruptured something inside me," she tells Andrey. "I'll see that child's face in every child I see." It is something Andrey can understand but Otto cannot. He wants Claire, and he is too absorbed in his own needs to believe Claire when she tells him that she is not ready for *any* man. He is convinced that she is rejecting him for Andrey, and threatens to kill the Russian: "If it'll be anyone," he warns Claire, "it'll be me."

But before Otto can do very much more than cast a pall on the talk and excitement, the glare of a flashlight pierces the darkness of the factory. Three soldiers dressed like Capuchin monks slowly make their way through the door, and, in German, order the huddled figures to put their hands in the air. When the soldiers want to know who they are and what they are doing in the factory, Jurek tells them, "We live around here, sir. Just having fun with couple girls." The deception is at least partially successful: while the men are shunted together in a corner of the factory, the "girls" are told to get out, to go home. Claire is reluctant to leave, and has to be pulled by Lini. Once outside, they begin to make their way toward the forest. Soon, they hear the sound of motors starting up but are afraid to look back. And then, "as though whips of wire had lashed their naked flesh without warning, both women screamed. From the factory, cutting through the motor sounds, had come the crack of several rifles."

Numb and weeping, Claire and Lini continue to stumble through the forest; they see nothing, know nothing, "except the ache in their hearts." But before they had gone very far they find themselves surrounded by twelve white-capped soldiers, and their tears of anguish turn to cries of fear. This time, however, the soldiers prove to be from the advancing Russian army; and *A Tale of One January* comes to an end with Claire and Lini being led to safety, their arms still around one another.

CHAPTER 9

Maltz Reestablished

I A New Start — Again

A Tale of One January is the shortest and, in many regards, the best of Maltz's five novels. Its merits were aptly defined by the reviewer for *Punch*, who wrote in the issue of January 18, 1967: "*A Tale of One January* is a short, harsh exciting story about ex-Auschwitz prisoners who escape from the column as it withdraws before the Russians. The characters of the two women and four men are both sweetly human and indurated by the horrors they have survived. It sustains the bleakness of events and grips the attention...." Other critics were just as enthusiastic. "It is a touching story, compassionately told," wrote the *Glasgow Herald's* reviewer, while the critic for the *Newcastle Journal* commented, "If Albert Maltz were not already known as a remarkable writer, the first two and a half pages of *A Tale of One January* would immediately establish him as one."[1]

Despite the praise bestowed upon *A Tale of One January* by the critics in Great Britain, the novel still has not been published in the United States. In this instance, however, the blacklist does not seem to have been an important factor, and there is a possibility that *One January* will yet appear with an American imprint. This is especially likely now that a new career — this time under his own name — once again seems to be under way for Maltz.

When Maltz returned to Los Angeles from Mexico in 1962, he continued to write film scripts with the use of a "front." But by the beginning of 1964 the blacklist had lost most of its effectiveness, and in 1967 Maltz began work on a script for Universal Studios with the understanding that he would be given full screen credit.

138

When *Two Mules for Sister Sara* was finally released in 1970, it was the first time in more than twenty years that Maltz's name had appeared on a film. And its somewhat preposterous title notwithstanding, *Two Mules* proved to be a critical *and* commercial success. ('' 'Two Mules for Sister Sara' . . . ought to be the realization of a movie lover's dream,'' wrote Roger Greenspun in *The New York Times*. ''And, by the happiest juxtaposition of imagination and talent, it is. I'm not sure that it is a great movie, but it is *very* good, and it stays and grows in the mind the way only movies of exceptional narrative intelligence do.''[2])

Equally important to the reestablishment of Maltz's career was the publication in July, 1968, of his short story, ''The Prisoner's Dog,'' by *The Saturday Evening Post;* this marked the first time that a story by Maltz under his own name was published in the United States since 1950. Three months later the *Post* published another story by Maltz, ''The Spoils of War,'' which it had rejected when the story had been submitted under a pseudonym in 1961.[3] And in 1970 Liveright published *Afternoon in the Jungle: The Selected Short Stories of Albert Maltz*. This volume, which includes eight previously published stories as well as one hitherto unpublished work, ''The Cop,''[4] not only was the first collection of Maltz's stories to be published in the United States since *The Way Things Are* came out in 1938; even more importantly, it was the first time since the blacklist had taken effect that *any* of Maltz's writings had been readily obtainable.[5]

II   A Final Word

Clearly, the time is now due for Maltz to be given the recognition that for so long has been denied him. When we hear of Maltz these days it almost always is in terms of his political commitments. More and more, he has come to be remembered as one of The Hollywood Ten — a writer who defied the House Committee on Un-American Activities, was sentenced to prison, then was blacklisted, and for almost twenty years was unable to put his own name on his work. But to remember Maltz solely in this way is to do him a great injustice.

Maltz, as I have attempted to show, was one of the pivotal figures in many of the most significant controversies that dominated the literary class wars of the 1930s and 1940s. He also was instrumental in establishing The Theatre Union and was one of the leaders in the struggle to counteract the virulent anti-Semitism of Father Coughlin. But, just as important, and not to be forgotten, is the fact that Albert Maltz was — and remains — a writer of great talent.

Surely, Maltz is one of the finest writers of social protest literature the United States has produced. Several of his short stories, most notably "Man on a Road" and "The Happiest Man in the World," are classic examples of protest literature. "Merry Go Round," though an unpolished work, remains a powerful drama of political corruption. And many of Maltz's novels are concerned with subjects with which few other writers have dealt: the Black Legion (*The Underground Stream*), racism and Fascism (*The Cross and the Arrow*), the concentration camp experience (*A Tale of One January*). These works retain a vitality and compassion that is absent from the works of writers of considerably greater reputation. Indeed, Maltz belongs in the company of such American writers of protest as James T. Farrell, Jack London, Upton Sinclair, John Steinbeck, and Richard Wright. All are read and discussed; all have a secure place in the history of American letters. Albert Maltz deserves no less.

Notes and References

Preface

1. Stanley J. Kunitz and Howard Haycraft, eds., *Twentieth Century Authors: A Biographical Dictionary of Modern Literature* (New York, 1942), p. 899.

2. Maltz to Jack Salzman, February 22, 1968. Hereafter, letters from Maltz to this writer will be designated Maltz to J.S.

3. William Phillips and Philip Rahv, "Literature in a Political Decade," *New Letters in America*, ed. Horace Gregory (New York, 1937), p. 170.

4. Waldo Frank, "Foreword," *American Writers' Congress*, ed. Henry Hart (New York, 1935), p. 5.

5. The speech has been frequently reprinted. It perhaps is most readily accessible in *Sinclair Lewis, The Man from Main Street: Selected Essays and Other Writings, 1904–1950*, ed. Harry E. Maule and Melville Cane, eds. (New York, 1953), pp. 3–17. The text of the address, entitled "The American Fear of Literature," is the second edition revised by Lewis.

6. Michael Gold, "Wilder: Prophet of the Genteel Christ," *New Republic*, LXIV (October 22, 1930), 266–267.

7. Edmund Wilson, "The Literary Class War," *New Republic*, LXX (May 4, 1932), 323. Part II of Wilson's article was published in *New Republic*, LXX (May 11, 1932), 347–349.

Chapter One

1. Baker, the prototype of Professor Hatcher in Thomas Wolfe's *Of Time and the River*, taught his '47 Workshop at Harvard from 1907 to 1925, and then taught at Yale. He died in 1935.

2. *Twentieth Century Authors*, p. 899.

3. Ibid.

4. See, for example, Joseph Wood Krutch, "A Political Melodrama," *Nation*, CXXXIV (May 11, 1932), 552–553.

5. Stark Young, "Cheery-Oh," *New Republic*, LXXI (June 1, 1932), 71.

6. Letter dated February 11, 1952. A copy of the letter was provided me by Albert Maltz.

7. Walker was mayor of New York City from 1925 until September, 1932, when he resigned and fled to Europe. He returned to the United States in 1940, and was appointed municipal arbiter for the garment industry by Mayor LaGuardia. He died six years later. For a consideration of the Seabury investigation, see Herbert Mitgang, *The Man Who Rode the Tiger* (Philadelphia, 1963).

8. In a conversation with this writer on October 5, 1968, Maltz commented that although "Merry Go Round" was based on an incident in Cleveland, he and Sklar did have the Walker administration in mind when they wrote the play. However, no direct parallels were drawn between the city officials and the characters in the play.

9. *Precedent,* a dramatization of the Tom Mooney case, was first produced on April 15, 1931.

10. Maltz to J.S., August 20, 1969.

11. "Merry Go Round" never has been published. A typescript of the play is among The Albert Maltz Papers at the Wisconsin Center for Theatre Research.

12. Both Maltz and George Sklar believe that "the frightfully grim ending [of "Merry Go Round"] for which there was no aesthetic catharsis" was also responsible for the poor audience (Maltz to J.S., August 20, 1969).

Chapter Two

1. The statement is from a publicity notice issued by The Theatre Union. The clipping, as well as other documents pertaining to The Theatre Union, is in the Theater Collection of The New York Public Library at Lincoln Center.

2. In addition to Maltz, Sklar, and Walker, the Executive Board of The Theatre Union included Michael Blankfort, Sylvia Fennington, Mary Fox, Samuel Friedman, Manuel Gomez, Margaret Larkin, Liston M. Oak, and Paul Peters.

3. "The Need for a Workers' Theatre," *Daily Worker,* December 16, 1933, p. 7.

4. Relatively little has been written about social drama of the 1930s. The best work on the Group Theatre is still Harold Clurman's *The Fervent Years* (New York, 1945). Hallie Flanagan's *Arena: The History of the Federal Theatre* (New York, 1940) can be supplemented by Jane De Hart Mathews, *The Federal Theatre 1935-1939: Plays, Relief, and Politics* (Princeton, 1967). Information about Artef is to be found in David S. Lifson, *The Yiddish Theatre in America* (New York, 1965). Three general studies are Gerald Rabkin, *Drama and Commitment: Politics in the American Theatre of the Thirties* (Bloomington, Ind., 1964), Morgan Himmelstein, *Drama Was a Weapon: The Left-Wing Theatre in New York 1929-1941* (New Brunswick, 1963) and Malcolm Goldstein, *The Political Stage: American Drama and the Theater of the Great Depression* (New York, 1974).

5. As yet there is no study of the Theatre Union. Documents pertaining to this organization can be found in The Theatre Union Collection of The New York Public Library and at the Wisconsin Center for Theatre Research.

6. Brecht's involvement with The Theatre Union is considered in Lee Baxandall, "Brecht in America, 1935," *The Drama Review,* II (Fall, 1967), 69–87.

7. Robert Forsythe [Kyle Crichton], "Wanted: A Theatre," *New Masses,* XXIX (October 18, 1938), 15.

8. See Eleanor Flexner, *American Playwrights 1918–1938* (New York, 1938), p. 288.

9. Albert Maltz and George Sklar, *Peace on Earth* (New York, 1934), p. 119. The published text of *Peace on Earth* contained an introduction by Sherwood Anderson.

10. The same technique was employed by many American playwrights of the time, including Elmer Rice (*Adding Machine*) and John Howard Lawson (*Processional*).

11. John Mason Brown, "The Play," *New York Post,* n.d., n.p.

12. Brooks Atkinson, "The Play," *New York Times,* November 30, 1933, p. 39.

13. Joseph Freeman, " 'Peace on Earth': The First Theatre Union Production," *Daily Worker,* December 2, 1933, p. 7.

14. John Howard Lawson, "Straight from the Shoulder," *New Theatre,* I (November, 1934), 11.

15. William Gardner, "The Theatre," *New Masses,* X (January 16, 1934), 29–30.

16. The aim of The Theatre Union and financial figures pertaining to the production of *Peace on Earth* are to be found in Margaret Larkin's letter to the drama editor of the *New York Times,* Sect. IX, March 18, 1934, p. 2.

17. Ibid.

18. According to Maltz, it was "the debacle of 'Mother' " that put The Theatre Union in a financial quagmire from which it was unable to extricate itself (Maltz to J.S., August 20, 1969).

19. See Himmelstein, *Drama Was a Weapon,* p. 57.

20. Rabkin, *Drama and Commitment,* p. 55.

21. Liston Oak, "Theatre Union Replies," *New Theatre,* I (November, 1934), 12.

22. Maltz to J.S., August 20, 1969.

23. In 1934, Maltz took a trip throughout the United States looking for information about Mother Bloor. Among the many miners whom he met was the brother of a man in West Virginia who had been imprisoned for taking part in a strike, and who, upon his release from jail, disavowed all union activities and would do nothing but play baseball. This provided Maltz with the base upon which to construct *Black Pit.*

24. *Black Pit* (New York, 1935), pp. 20–21. Upon rereading the printed text after many years, Maltz decided that he would make two changes in the text were it to be reprinted: In describing a character he would specify the type of accent the character had; and he would "make the spelling more normal while keeping the locutions and grammar of the character" (Maltz to J.S., April 25, 1969).

25. For a brief consideration of the sectarian response to *Black Pit,* see Rabkin, pp. 59–60.

26. *New York Times,* March 21, 1935, p. 26.

27. *Nation,* CXL (April 3, 1935), 400.

28. *New Masses,* XV (April 2, 1935), 42.

29. Not all the reviews of *Black Pit* were unfavorable. See, for example, Stark Young, "Of Blackest Midnight Born," *New Republic,* LXXXII (April 17, 1935), 289.

30. Maltz to J.S., June 20, 1969.

31. Atkinson, *New York Times,* March 21, 1935, p. 26.

32. "Red Head Baker" was included in *One Hundred Non-Royalty Radio Plays* (New York, 1941).

33. In 1957–58, Maltz completed two versions of a play about Victor Hugo. Neither version fully satisfied him, and it was not until 1969 that Maltz was able to make the desired changes. As of this date, however, the play has not been produced.

Chapter Three

1. *The Way Things Are* (New York, 1938). Until the publication in 1970 of *Afternoon in the Jungle,* this was the only collection of Maltz's stories published in the United States. (In 1960, all of Maltz's stories, with the exception of "The Cop," were collected under the title, *Abseits von Broadway,* which was published in East Germany.)

2. Fred T. Marsh, "Albert Maltz's Stories," *New York Times Book Review,* July 24, 1938, p. 6.

3. See, for example, Clifton Fadiman's comments about "Season of Celebration" in the *New Yorker,* XIV (April 30, 1938), 59, and Alfred Kazin's review of *The Way Things Are,* "Youth or the End of the Parade?" *New York Herald Tribune Books,* July 24, 1938, p. 2.

4. Kazin, "Youth," p. 2.

5. A brief consideration of this genre is to be found in Walter Rideout, *The Radical Novel in the United States, 1900–1950* (Cambridge, Mass., 1956). It should be noted, however, that Rideout inexplicably omits Tom Kromer's *Waiting for Nothing* from this category but includes Henry Roth's *Call It Sleep.*

6. "Man on a Road" first appeared in *New Masses,* XIV (January 8, 1935), 19–21; in the same year, it was included in *Proletarian Literature in the United States,* ed. Granville Hicks, et. al. (New York, 1935). Subsequent to its inclusion in *The Way Things Are,* "Man on a Road" has been

reprinted many times, most recently in Joseph North, ed., *New Masses: An Anthology of the Rebel Thirties* (New York, 1969) and Daniel Aaron and Robert Bendiner, eds., *The Strenuous Decade: A Social and Intellectual Record of the 1930s* (New York, 1970).

7. See Michael Gold's Introduction to *The Way Things Are,* p. 14.

8. Edward J. O'Brien, ed., *Best Short Stories of 1936* (Boston, 1936), p. xxiii.

9. The story was first published in *The Way Things Are.*

10. "The Game" originally was published in *Scribner's Magazine,* C (December, 1936), 36–38.

11. "Good-by" first appeared in *New Masses,* XXI (December 15, 1936), 37–40; "The Drop-Forge Man" was first published in *The Way Things Are.*

12. "Incident on a Street Corner" was first printed in the *New Yorker,* XIII (November 27, 1937), 22–23.

13. "A Letter from the Country" originally was published in *New Masses,* XXIV (August 17, 1937), 16–18. The narrator, Lester Cooley, reappears in Maltz's *The Journey of Simon McKeever.*

14. Since its initial appearance in *Harper's,* CLXXVII (June, 1938), 74–79, "The Happiest Man on Earth" frequently has been reprinted. Most recently, it has been included in Louis Filler, ed., *The Anxious Years: America in the 1930s* (New York, 1964) and Jack Salzman, ed., *Years of Protest: A Collection of American Writings of the 1930s* (New York, 1967).

15. Michael Gold, Introduction to *The Way Things Are,* p. 13.

Chapter Four

1. For a study of some of the more significant demagogues — including Father Charles E. Coughlin — see David H. Bennett, *Demagogues in the Depression: American Radicals and the Union Party, 1931–1936* (New Brunswick, 1969).

2. Quoted in the *New York Times,* May 27, 1966, p. 26.

3. Quoted in James P. Shenton, "Fascism and Father Coughlin," *Wisconsin Magazine of History,* XLIV (Autumn, 1960), 9.

4. *New York Times,* May 27, 1966.

5. A copy of the "Preamble and Principles of the National Union for Social Justice" was printed on the overside of all application forms for membership in the National Union for Social Justice. The Preamble and Principles have been included in my introduction to the reprint edition of *Equality* (Westport, Conn., 1970).

6. Shenton, p. 8.

7. "Foreword," *American Writers' Congress.*

8. *"We Hold these TRUTHS . . . "* (New York, 1939), p. 9.

9. Beginning with the sixth issue (October, 1939), the masthead of

Equality read: "An Independent, Non-Sectarian, Monthly Journal to Defend Democratic Rights and Combat Racial and Religious Intolerance."

10. James Wechsler, "The Coughlin Terror," *Nation,* CXLIX (July 22, 1939), 92.

11. Wechsler, p. 95.

12. The review of *Gone with the Wind,* entitled "Four Million Dollars Worth of Wind," appeared in the February, 1940, issue; Steinbeck's novel was reviewed in the next issue (March), and *Native Son* was reviewed in the issue of June, 1940.

13. Letter from Harold Croy to this writer, May 20, 1969.

14. In a letter to this writer dated October 26, 1969, Maltz noted that it was essential to "avoid equating the end of the literature of social protest with the dissolution of the political left," since it was not until 1947 "that the C.P. started on its path of dissolution."

15. A list of many of the novels written during this period is to be found in Rideout, *The Radical Novel,* pp. 295–298.

16. The Studs Lonigan trilogy was published between 1932 and 1935. *Pity Is Not Enough,* the first novel in Ms. Herbst's trilogy, was published in 1933; it was followed by *The Executioner Waits* (1934) and *Rope of Gold* (1939).

17. "Editorial Statement," *Partisan Review,* I (February-March, 1934), 2.

18. "Foreword," *American Writers' Congress.*

19. "Call for an American Writers' Congress," *New Masses,* XIV (January 22, 1935), 20.

20. James T. Farrell, *A Note on Literary Criticism* (New York, 1936), p. 32.

21. James T. Farrell, "Theatre Chronicle," *Partisan Review and Anvil,* III (February, 1936), 29.

22. Michael Gold, "Papa Anvil and Mother Partisan," *New Masses,* XVIII (February 18, 1936), 22.

23. Edmund Wilson, "Novelist Bites Critic," *Nation,* CXLII (June 24, 1936), 808.

24. William Phillips, "Marking Time," *New Masses,* XXI (December 22, 1936), 23.

25. For a history of *Partisan Review,* see James Gilbert, *Writers and Partisans: A History of Literary Radicalism in America* (New York, 1968).

26. "Editorial Statement," *Partisan Review,* IV (December, 1937), 4.

27. Ibid.

28. Gilbert, *Writers and Partisans,* pp. 157–158.

29. Granville Hicks, "On Leaving the Communist Party," *New Republic,* C (October 4, 1939), 244.

Chapter Five

1. Alfred Kazin, "Here Is a Left-Wing Writer Who Can Write," *New*

York Herald Tribune Books, June 30, 1940, p. 5.

2. For a succinct discussion of the development of unions during the 1930s, see Dixon Wechter, *The Age of the Great Depression 1929-1941* (New York, 1948), pp. 107-122.

3. Albert Maltz, "Bodies by Fisher," *New Masses,* XXIII (January 26, 1937), 25-26. Reprinted in North, ed., *New Masses,* pp. 107-122.

4. See Kenneth T. Jackson, *The Ku Klux Klan in the City 1915-1930* (New York, 1967), pp. 142-143; Morris Janowitz, "Black Legions on the March," *America in Crisis: Fourteen Crucial Episodes in American History,* ed. Daniel Aaron (New York, 1951), pp. 305-325; Wechter, *Great Depression,* p. 164.

5. Maltz to J.S., July 24, 1969.

6. Harold Straus, *"The Underground Stream* and Other Fiction," *New York Times Book Review,* July 7, 1940, p. 7.

7. George Sklar gave Maltz a copy of *Man's Fate* in October, 1935. However, in a letter to this writer dated August 12, 1969, Maltz wrote that although he had carefully studied the style of Malraux's novel, he was convinced that his characterization of Grebb was not influenced by Ferrel.

8. In a letter dated August 20, 1969, Maltz wrote: "The similarity between Paul Turner in 'The Underground Stream' and my father's lead poisoning was indeed quite conscious."

9. While in Flint, Michigan, Maltz learned that the head of the State Police had "boned up in Marxist literature so he could talk the Communist lingo to men he arrested in his attempts to win some of them to be informers for him" (Maltz to J.S., August 12, 1969).

10. Lewis Gannet, "Books and Things," *New York Herald Tribune,* June 26, 1940, p. 23.

11. Michael Gold, "Review," *Daily Worker,* July 16, 1940, p. 7.

12. Ralph Thompson, "Books of the Times," *New York Times,* July 8, 1940, p. 15.

13. Louis Filler, "Party Business," *Saturday Review of Literature,* XXII (July 13, 1940), 18.

14. Harry Hansen, "The First Reader," *New York World Telegram,* June 26, 1940.

15. Kazin, "A Writer with Talent," *New York Herald Tribune,* June 30, 1940, p. 5.

16. "Sunday Morning on Twentieth Street" first appeared in *Southern Review,* V (1940), 469-477; "Afternoon in the Jungle" was originally published in *New Yorker,* XVI (January 11, 1941), 17-20.

17. Chester Eisinger, "Character and Self in Fiction on the Left," *Proletarian Writers of the Thirties,* ed. David Madden (Carbondale, Ill., 1968), p. 171.

Chapter Six

1. For a study of these novels, see Joseph J. Waldmeir, *American*

Novels of the Second World War (Hague, 1969).

2. Maltz to J.S., July 24, 1969.

3. Ibid.

4. Ibid.

5. Ibid.

6. Ibid.

7. Eberhard Brüning, *Albert Maltz: Ein Amerikanischer Arbeiter-schriftsteller* (Halle [Saale], 1957), p. 101.

8. Samuel Sillen, "Profile of a German Worker," *New Masses,* LIII (October 3, 1944), 23.

9. Orville Prescott, "Books of the Time, *New York Times,* September 22, 1944, p. 17.

10. George F. Whicher, "Books and Things," *New York Herald Tribune,* September 18, 1944, p. 15.

11. Chester E. Eisinger, *Fiction of the Forties* (Chicago, 1963), p. 50.

12. Isidor Schneider, "Probing Writers' Problems," *New Masses,* LVII (October 23, 1945), 22–25.

13. "What Shall We Ask of Writers?" *New Masses,* LVIII (February 12, 1946), 19–22.

14. Frank, "Foreword," *American Writers' Congress,* p. 5.

15. Albert Maltz, "The Citizen Writer," *The Citizen Writer* (New York, 1950), pp. 7–10.

16. Daniel Aaron, *Writers on the Left: Episodes in American Literary Criticism* (New York, 1961), pp. 386–387.

17. Isidor Schneider, "Background to Error," *New Masses,* LVIII (February 12, 1946), 23–25.

18. For a discussion of the Left's attitude toward MacLeish, see Aaron, *Writers on the Left,* pp. 264–267, and Salzman, ed., *Years of Protest,* pp 238–244.

19. Howard Fast, "Art and Politics," *New Masses,* LVIII (Feburary 26, 1946), 6–8.

20. Joseph North, "No Retreat for the Writer," *New Masses,* LVIII (February 26, 1946), 8–10.

21. Alvah Bessie, "What Is Freedom for Writers?" *New Masses,* LVIII (March 12, 1946), 8–10.

22. John Howard Lawson, "Art Is a Weapon," *New Masses,* LVIII (March 19, 1946), 18–20.

23. "Moving Forward," *New Masses,* LIX (April 9, 1946), 8–10, 21.

24. "Hollywood Writers Send Messages to Art Forum," *Daily Worker,* April 19, 1946, p. 12.

25. Rideout, *Radical Novel,* p. 322.

26. Aaron, *Writers on the Left,* p. 386.

27. David Shannon, *The Decline of American Communism: A History of the Communist Party in the United States Since 1945* (New York, 1959), p. 57.

28. George Charney, *A Long Journey* (Chicago, 1968), p. 183.

29. Alfred Kazin, *On Native Grounds: An Interpretation of Modern American Prose Literature* (New York, 1942), p. 382.

30. Walter Goodman, *The Committee: The Extraordinary Career of the House Committee on Un-American Activities* (New York, 1968), p. 173.

31. Ibid., p. 203.

32. Robert K. Carr, *The House Committee on Un-American Activities 1945-1950* (Ithaca, 1952), p. 54.

33. Quoted in Carr, p. 58.

34. Quoted in Carr, p. 60.

35. See Goodman, pp. 204-207; Carr, p. 42.

36. Part of Brecht's testimony before the Committee is reprinted in Gordon Kahn, *Hollywood on Trial: The Story of the 10 Who Were Indicted* (New York, 1948), pp. 121-129. There is a recording of Brecht's testimony, "Bertolt Brecht Before the Committee on Un-American Activities."

37. The Hollywood Ten became The Hollywood Nine when Edward Dmytryk became a "friendly" witness shortly after completing his prison term.

38. Alvah Bessie, *Inquisition in Eden* (New York, 1965), p. 6.

39. See Kahn, pp. 70-71.

40. Kahn, p. 85.

41. The text of "The Writer as the Conscience of the People" was printed in Maltz's *The Citizen Writer: Essays in Defense of American Culture* (New York, 1950), pp. 11-20.

42. The unread statements by Lawson and Trumbo are printed in Kahn, pp. 72-77 and 82-85. Two works by Trumbo offer valuable insights into The Hollywood Ten affair: *Time of the Toad: A Study of Inquisition in America* (Hollywood, 1949) and *Additional Dialogue: Letters of Dalton Trumbo, 1942-1965,* ed. Helen Manfull (New York, 1970).

43. The entire statement is included in Kahn, *Hollywood on Trial,* pp. 87-90.

44. *PM,* October 22, 1947. Quoted in Carr, *House Committee,* p. 55.

45. Kahn, p. 132.

46. Quoted in Kahn, "Foreword."

47. Kahn, pp. 141-144.

48. The resolution of the Hollywood executives, which was announced by Dore Schary, became known as the Waldorf Statement.

49. See Goodman, *The Committee,* p. 221.

50. Ibid.

51. *Hollywood on Trial,* p. 164.

52. See Kahn, pp. 176-177.

53. Maltz to J.S., December 29, 1969.

54. The Committee also was castigated in the editorial pages of the *New York Times, Washington Post,* and *Detroit Free Press* (see Goodman, p. 220).

55. Quoted in Goodman, p. 223.

56. The address, entitled "Books Are on Trial in America," was reprinted in *The Citizen Writer,* pp. 43–48.

57. *On the Eve of Prison: Two Addresses by Gale Sondergaard and Albert Maltz* (Hollywood, 1950), p. 9.

Chapter Seven

1. Stevenson's endeavor to seat himself in Maltz's car is described in *The Journey of Simon McKeever* (Boston, 1949), p. 152.

2. Maltz to J.S., December 4, 1969. This letter is the source for all comments that pertain to Stevenson.

3. Inside the house, Maltz happened upon a palsied man who was reading Havelock Ellis's *Dance of Life;* it is this book that Simon McKeever carries with him on his journey.

4. *Simon McKeever,* p. 231.

5. In *The Journey of Simon McKeever,* this became the Finney Home.

6. William DuBois, "Tale of a 'Spunky Septuagenarian,' " *New York Times Book Review,* May 8, 1949, p. 5.

7. See, for example, Lewis Gannett, "Books and Things," *New York Herald Tribune,* May 16, 1949, p. 13; Milton Rugoff, "Pilgrim — and a Message," *New York Herald Tribune Weekly Book Review,* May 15, 1949, p. 8.

8. Maltz used the same name in "A Letter from the Country."

9. In addition to the reviews by DuBois and Gannett, see Josephine Lawrence, "Relief in Calif.," *Saturday Review of Literature,* XXXII (May 7, 1949), 17; Joseph Schiffman, "Simple Simon Finds a World," *Brooklyn Daily Eagle,* May 29, 1949.

10. Reported in *Variety,* April 13, 1949.

11. Ibid.

12. In 1962, the rights to *The Journey of Simon McKeever* were sold to a film producer, who failed to get financing for the project. As of this writing, a film corporation, Commonwealth, owns the film rights to *Journey,* as well as the film script which Maltz made of it.

13. *New York Herald Tribune,* May 16, 1949, p. 13. *The Nation* commented in part: " 'The Journey of Simon McKeever' is a simple story of an old man, his troubles and problems. It is not a propaganda novel nor does it make explicit social or political points. By suppressing it the motion-picture industry confirms the charge made at the time of the Thomas committee hearings that their real purpose was to impose a censorship on the industry" (168 [May 14, 1949], 543).

14. Maltz continued to visit Stevenson on a fairly regular basis until The Hollywood Ten case made such visits impossible; by the time Maltz completed his prison term, Stevenson had died.

15. Maltz to J.S., February 14, 1970.

16. "Circus Come to Town," *Masses & Mainstream,* III (July, 1950), 33–45.

17. Maltz to J.S., February 14, 1970.

Chapter Eight

1. Maltz to J.S., December 4, 1969. Unless otherwise noted, this letter is the source of all information pertaining to Maltz's activities at this time.

2. "The Whiskey Men," *Masses & Mainstream,* IV (November, 1951), 43–44.

3. Maltz to J.S., February 14, 1970. "The Morrison Case" never has been published in the United States; a typescript of the play was provided me by Albert Maltz.

4. Maltz to J.S., December 5, 1969.

5. Although Maltz quickly finished a first draft of the novel, he was dissatisfied with it and wrote two different drafts of the work before sending it to a publisher (Maltz to J.S., August 11, 1970).

6. In a letter dated December 4, 1969, Maltz wrote the following about Floyd Varney: "Floyd Varney was based in part upon a man who had just received a sentence of 35 years to life and who told me that he had considered suicide, but had rejected it. The suicide was based upon an actual suicide while I was there: a newly arrested man, who had served time before, slashed his wrists with a piece of glass he picked up in one of our infrequent hours in an outside enclosure."

7. *Denver Post,* November 28, 1919. Quoted in Robert Elias, *Theodore Dreiser: Apostle of Nature* (Ithaca, 1970), p. 223.

8. *A Long Day in a Short Life* (New York, 1957), pp. 207–208.

9. *Afro-American,* July 6, 1957, p. 2.

10. *Pittsburgh Courier,* July 27, 1957.

11. *New York Times,* International Edition, June 22, 1953, pp. 1 and 6.

12. Ibid., p. 6.

13. Maltz to J.S., December 9, 1969.

14. See Murray Schumach, *The Face on the Cutting Room Floor: The Story of Movie and Television Censorship* (New York, 1964), p. 130.

15. Ibid., pp. 131–132.

16. In addition to the account of blacklisting to be found in *The Face on the Cutting Room Floor,* see Elizabeth Poe, "The Hollywood Story: The Technique of the Purge," *Frontier* (May, 1954), 6–25; the Fall-Winter, 1970, issue of *Film Culture,* which is devoted to blacklisting in Hollywood.

17. Schumach, *Cutting Room Floor,* p. 120.

18. "Wrong-Way Frank," *Journal American,* March 22, 1960.

19. "Note to Sinatra," *Journal American,* March 28, 1960.

20. "A Statement from Frank Sinatra," *Hollywood Reporter,* March 28, 1960.

21. One of the few public statements in support of Sinatra's hiring of Maltz was voiced in a New York *Post* editorial, "An Oscar to Sinatra," which said in part: "Frank Sinatra has joined the select company of Hollywood valiants who have declared their independence from the Un-American Activities Committee and the American Legion. He has hired Albert Maltz, once jailed for contempt of Congress, to write a film adaptation for an upcoming picture.... We hope men of lesser courage in the film colony will come out of their bomb shelters into the fresh air soon. Meanwhile, an Oscar to Sinatra."

22. "Statement," *New York Times,* April 12, 1960, p. 28.

23. Maltz to J.S., June 3, 1969. Maltz cites Howard Fast as a blacklisted writer who "continued to publish under his own name, albeit by means of establishing his own publishing house."

24. Ibid.

25. Under the title, "The Prisoner's Dog," "Pani" was published in the *Saturday Evening Post,* II (July 13, 1968), 48–53.

26. Julian Silva [Albert Maltz], "With Laughter," *Southwest Review,* XLV (Spring, 1960), 144–155.

27. The story was "Husband and Wife"; it was produced in 1962 as "The Great Alberti."

28. The source material for *A Tale of One January* is in the Library of Columbia University.

Chapter Nine

1. *Glasgow Herald,* January 21, 1967; *Newcastle Journal,* January 14, 1967.

2. *New York Times,* June 25, 1970, p. 55.

3. "The Spoils of War," *Saturday Evening Post,* #20 (October 5, 1968), 65–66, 70–72.

4. In addition to "The Cop," the stories include: "Man on a Road," "The Way Things Are," "The Happiest Man on Earth," "Sunday Morning on Twentieth Street," "Afternoon in the Jungle," "Circus Come to Town," "With Laughter," "The Farmer's Dog."

5. For several years, a reprint of *The Cross and the Arrow* has been listed in *Paperback Books in Print,* but this edition is very difficult to locate in bookstores.

Selected Bibliography

PRIMARY SOURCES

1. *Plays* (Arranged in order of publication)

Peace on Earth. New York: Samuel French, 1934.
Black Pit. New York: G. P. Putnam's Sons, 1935.
"Private Hicks," *New Theatre,* II (November, 1935), 20–25. Reprinted in
    William Kozlenko, ed., *The Best Short Plays of the Social Theatre.*
    New York: Random House, 1939.
"Rehearsal," *One Act Play Magazine,* I (March, 1938), 994–1020.
"Red Head Baker," *One Hundred Non-Royalty Radio Plays,* ed. William
    Kozlenko. New York: Greenberg, 1941.

2. *Stories*

A. Collected
The Way Things Are. New York: International Publishers, 1938. (Includes
    "Season of Celebration," "Good-by," "Incident on a Street Cor-
    ner," "The Game," "A Letter from the Country," "The Drop-Forge
    Man," "The Way Things Are," "Man on a Road.")
Afternoon in the Jungle: The Selected Short Stories of Albert Maltz. New
    York: Liveright, 1971. (Includes "Man on a Road," "The Way
    Things Are," "The Happiest Man on Earth," "Sunday Morning on
    Twentieth Street," "Afternoon in the Jungle," "Circus Come to
    Town," "With Laughter," "The Farmer's Dog," "The Cop.")

B. Uncollected
"The Spoils of War," *The Saturday Evening Post,* #20 (October 5, 1968),
    65–66, 70–72.

3. *Novels* (Arranged in order of publication)

The Underground Stream. Boston: Little, Brown and Co., 1940.
The Cross and the Arrow. Boston: Little, Brown and Co., 1944.
The Journey of Simon McKeever. Boston: Little, Brown and Co., 1949.
A Long Day in a Short Life. New York: International Publishers, 1957.
A Tale of One January. London: Calder and Boyers, 1966.

153

4. *Nonfiction*

A. Collected

The Citizen Writer: Essays in Defense of American Culture. New York:
International Publishers, 1950. (Includes "The Citizen Writer," "The
Writer as the Conscience of the People," "Testament," "The Amer-
ican Artist and the American Tradition," "The Verdict of History,"
"The Anti-American Conspiracy," "Books Are on Trial in
America.")

B. Uncollected (A selected list arranged in order of publication)

"The Need for a Workers' Theatre," *Daily Worker,* X (December 16,
1933), 7.

" 'Have Faith in Your Leaders' Was Plea to Toledo A.F.L. Chiefs," *Daily
Worker,* XI (June 7, 1934), 5.

"Cattle in the Gravel Pits," *New Masses,* XII (July 24, 1934), 14–16.

"Current New Theatre," *Daily Worker,* XI (September 7, 1934), 5.

"In the Wake of the Drought," *Social Work Today,* November 2, 1934.

"Boston Back Door Censorship Used Against Stevedore," *Daily Worker,*
XII (September 26, 1935), 5.

"Change the World," *Daily Worker,* XII (December 30, 1935), 7.

"Change the World," *Daily Worker,* XII (December 31, 1935), 7.

"Bodies by Fischer," *New Masses,* XXIII (January 26, 1937), 25–26.

"Marching Song," *"New Theatre & Film,* IV (March, 1937), 13, 56.

"Introduction," *"We hold these TRUTHS . . . ": Statements on anti-
Semitism by 54 leading American writers, statesmen, educators,
clergymen and trade-unionists.* New York: The League of American
Writers, 1939. (This pamphlet also includes a statement by Maltz on
anti-Semitism [pp. 70–71].)

"To All People of Good Will," *Equality,* I (May, 1939), 3–5.

"Four Million Dollars Worth of Wind," *Equality,* II (February, 1940), 18,
33.

"Grapes of Wrath Folk: An Oppressed Minority," *Equality,* II (March,
1940), 17, 35.

"The Meaning of Native Son," *Equality,* II (June, 1940), 35.

"What Shall We Ask of Writers?" *New Masses,* LVIII (February 12,
1946), 19–22.

"Moving Forward," *New Masses,* LIX (April 9, 1946), 8–10, 21.

"On the Eve of Prison," *On the Eve of Prison: Two Addresses by Gale
Sondergaard and Albert Maltz.* Hollywood, 1950.

"Open Letter to *The Saturday Evening Post* on Edward Dmytryk," *Hollywood Reporter,* 1951.

"The Whiskey Men," *Masses & Mainstream,* IV (November, 1951),
42–47.

"Some Biographical Data of My Life," *Zietschrift für Anglistik und
Amerikanistik,* II (1953), 129–130.

SECONDARY SOURCES

AARON, DANIEL. *Writers on the Left: Episodes in American Literary Communism.* New York: Harcourt, Brace & World, 1961. Discusses the controversy arising from Maltz's answer to the question, "What Shall We Ask of Writers?" Sees Maltz as a writer "who suffered a serious ideological collapse but was nursed back to regularity by solicitous comrades."

BAXANDALL, LEE. "Brecht in America, 1935," *The Drama Review,* XII (Fall, 1967), 69–87. An account of The Theatre Union's production of Brecht's *Mother;* includes personal recollections by Maltz and other members of The Theatre Union.

BESSIE, ALVAH. *Inquisition in Eden.* New York: Macmillan, 1965. Written by one of The Hollywood Ten, this account of the Hollywood witch hunts centers on the Ten. Part of Maltz's testimony before the House Committee on Un-American Activities is reprinted, and the Sinatra-*Slovik* incident is considered briefly.

BIBERMAN, HERBERT. *Salt of the Earth: The Story of a Film.* Boston: Beacon Press, 1965. Biberman's account of his efforts to film and then distribute *Salt of the Earth* includes several pages devoted to The Hollywood Ten episode.

BLAKE, BEN. *The Awakening of the American Theatre.* New York: Tomorrow, 1935. A monograph on the development of social drama in the 1930s; *Peace on Earth* is seen as a seminal work in the growth of the New Theatre Movement.

BRÜNING, EBERHARD. *Albert Maltz.* Halle, East Germany: Veb Max Niemeyer Verlag, 1957. The only full-length study of Maltz to date, this work, by an East German scholar and friend of Maltz, never has been translated into English.

_____. *Das Amerikanische Drama Der Dreissiger Jahre.* Berlin: Rutten & Loening, 1966. A detailed study of the social drama of the 1930s, which considers all of Maltz's plays of the period.

CARR, ROBERT K. *The House Committee on Un-American Activities.* Ithaca: Cornell University Press, 1952. Pages 55–57 are devoted to the Hollywood Hearings; Carr concludes that the Committee "failed to demonstrate that Hollywood was a hotbed of Communist activity...."

CHARNEY, GEORGE. *A Long Journey.* Chicago: Quadrangle, 1968. A memoir by a former member of the Communist Party. The "What Shall We Ask of Writers?" episode is discussed as an example of how "a form of witch-hunting developed in defense of ideology that warped [the Communist Party's] approach to people and ideas."

EISINGER, CHESTER E. *Fiction of the Forties.* Chicago: University of Chicago Press, 1963. In *The Cross and the Arrow,* "Maltz puts his faith in the endurance of human dignity and also, perhaps, in the essential right-mindedness of the proletariat."

———. "Character and Self in Fiction on the Left," *Proletarian Writers of the Thirties,* ed. David Madden. Carbondale: Southern Illinois University Press, 1968. Contends that Maltz illustrates "the ambiguous relationship between society and self forced upon the leftist writer by his ideological preconceptions.

Film Culture, #50–51 (Fall & Winter, 1970). The entire issue of this double number of *Film Culture,* guest-edited by Gordon Hitchens, is devoted to Hollywood blacklisting. Included are interviews, segments of the Hollywood Hearings, and photos of The Hollywood Ten.

FLEXNER, ELEANOR. *American Playwrights: 1918–1938.* New York: Simon and Schuster, 1938. Many of the leading playwrights of the 1920s and 1930s are measured against the yardstick of social concern and are found wanting. The study includes a brief consideration of *Merry Go Round* and *Peace on Earth.*

GOLDSTEIN, MALCOLM. *The Political Stage: American Drama and Theater of the Great Depression.* New York: Oxford University Press, 1974. Chapter 2 of this excellent study is concerned with "The Theater Union 1933–1935"; Chapter 8 deals with "The Theater Union 1935–1937 and Related Companies." This is the most accurate and detailed account of the Theatre Union to date.

GOODMAN, WALTER. *The Committee: The Extraordinary Career of the House Committee on Un-American Activities.* New York: Farrar, Straus, and Giroux, 1968. Discusses the Hollywood Hearings, and concludes that they "brought forth no heroes."

GURKO, LEO. *The Angry Decade: American Literature and Thought from 1929 to Pearl Harbor.* 1940; rpt. New York: Harper Colophon, 1968. Briefly considers *The Underground Stream* and *The Cross and the Arrow.* Sees Maltz as "an illustration of how talent, if sufficiently vital, can survive any thesis superimposed upon it."

HIMMELSTEIN, MORGAN. *Drama Was a Weapon: The Left-Wing Theatre in New York, 1929–1941.* New Brunswick: Rutgers University Press, 1963. In addition to a chapter devoted to The Theatre Union, this not always trustworthy study includes references to *Merry Go Round* and "Private Hicks."

KAHN, GORDON. *Hollywood on Trial: The Story of the Ten Who Were Indicted.* New York: Boni & Gaer, 1948. Written with the collaboration of The Hollywood Ten, this account of the Hollywood Hearings reprints large segments of the exchange between the Committee members and the Ten.

LUCCOCK, HALFORD E. *American Mirror: Social, Ethical and Religious Aspects of American Literature 1930–1940.* New York: Macmillan, 1940. Includes a brief consideration of *Black Pit, Peace on Earth,* "Season of Celebration," and "The Happiest Man on Earth"; the latter is seen as one of the most notable of the many sharp, scathing stories about the years of unemployment.

NANNES, CASPAR H. *Politics in the American Drama.* Washington, D.C.: The Catholic University of America Press, 1960. *Merry Go Round* is briefly discussed as a "fast moving and exciting" play of gangsters and politics.

POE, ELIZABETH. "The Hollywood Story," *Frontier* (May, 1954), 6–25. An account of the Hollywood purge.

RABKIN, GERALD. *Drama and Commitment: Politics in the American Theatre of the Thirties.* Bloomington: Indiana University Press, 1964. Chapter III, "Theatre Union: Theatre as a Weapon," contains a discussion of *Peace on Earth* and *Black Pit.*

RIDEOUT, WALTER B. *The Radical Novel in the United States, 1900–1954: Some Interrelations of Literature and Society.* Cambridge, Mass.: Harvard University Press, 1956. Discusses *The Underground Stream,* which is seen as an historically important novel — despite its confusion between ideology and belief — "because it initiated the whole series of books chiefly concerned with an examination of the Communist's personality and faith or with a depiction of his life as the only fully admirable mode of existence available in the United States today."

SALZMAN, JACK. "The Way Things Were: Hoover, Maltz, and the Literary Left," *Journal of Human Relations,* XV (Third Quarter, 1967), 37–50. A consideration of the works Maltz wrote during the 1930s.

SCHUMACH, MURRAY. *The Face on the Cutting Room Floor: The Story of Movie and Television Censorship.* New York: William Morrow, 1964. Chapter 4, "Aftermath of Cowardice," includes a discussion of both the Sinatra-*Slovik* affair and "The Battle of the Unfriendly Ten."

SHANNON, DAVID A. *The Decline of American Communism: A History of the Communist Party of the United States Since 1945.* New York: Harcourt, Brace, 1959. Contains a harshly worded account of the "What Shall We Ask of Writers?" episode.

TRUMBO, DALTON. *Time of the Toad: A Study of Inquisition in America.* Hollywood: The Hollywood Ten, 1949. Much of this pamphlet, which was sponsored by The Hollywood Ten, is devoted to the Hollywood Hearings.

———. *Additional Dialogue: Letters of Dalton Trumbo, 1942–1962,* ed. Helen Manfull. New York: M. Evans, 1970. Includes four letters to Maltz; altogether, an invaluable source for an understanding of The Hollywood Ten.

Index

(The works of Albert Maltz are listed under his name)

Aaron, Daniel, 86, 93
Afraid to Talk, 21, 22
Algren, Nelson, 34
Alper, Michael, 47
American Tragedy, An (Dreiser), 121–22
Atkinson, Brooks, 27, 31
Ausubel, Nathan, 47

Baker, George, 15
Beckett, Samuel, 35
Bessie, Alvah, 91–92, 97, 98, 101
Biberman, Herbert, 97, 101, 103
Bitter Stream (Wolfson), 23
Black Legion, The, 57
Blankfort, Michael, 73
Bower, Ruth, 43
Brecht, Bertolt, 97
Brown, John Mason, 27

Calmer, Alan, 51
Charney, George, 93–94
Cole, Lester, 97, 101
Cooper, Gary, 97
Coughlin, Charles E., 45–47
Coy, Harold, 47, 48

Dahlberg, Edward, 34
Dean, Alexander, 15
Deutsch, Albert, 47
Dies, Martin, 95
Dmytryk, Edward, 97, 101, 103
Dupee, Fred, 52

Ehrenbourg, Ilya, 75
Eisinger, Chester, 69
Equality, 46–48
Execution of Private Slovik, The (Huei), 130, 131

Farrell, James T., 50, 51, 52, 90, 92
Fast, Howard, 53, 91
Fearing, Kenneth, 90
Filler, Louis, 69
For Whom the Bell Tolls (Hemingway), 73
Forsythe, Robert, 24
Frank, Waldo, 46, 50
Freeman, Joseph, 27

Gannett, Lewis, 68, 115–16
Gardner, William, 28
Gilbert, James, 52–53
Gold, Michael, 43–44, 50, 51, 53, 68, 72
Gone with the Wind, 47
Goodman, Walter, 96
Gorki, Maxim, 33–34, 35, 107

Hansen, Harry, 69
Hemingway, Ernest, 40, 73
Hicks, Granville, 51, 53
Hollywood Ten, The, 95–103, 115, 116, 117

Iceman Cometh, The (O'Neill), 35
I'll Take My Stand, 72

Jackson, Marjorie, 126
Johnny Got His Gun (Trumbo), 53

Kafka, Franz, 107
Kahn, Gordon, 101–102, 128
Kazin, Alfred, 34, 69, 94
Kennedy, John F., 130
Krutch, Joseph Wood, 31

Lardner, Ring, Jr., 97, 101
Larkin, Margaret, 24

Lawson, John Howard, 28, 92, 97, 98, 99, 101, 103
Lerner, Max, 100
Let Freedom Ring (Bein), 23
Lewis, John L. 54–55

Macdonald, Dwight, 52
Maltz, Albert: addresses rally for Civil and Human Rights, 103; adopts pseudonym, 132; attacked by Left, 85–95; attends Yale, 15; cited for contempt by HUAC, 101–102; delivers address at Conference on Thought Control in U.S., 98; encounter with Sinatra, 129–31; goes to Hollywood, 72; imprisoned, 117; joins Theatre Union, 22; meets Sklar, 15; publication of "What Shall We Ask of Writers?"; reads statement to HUAC; released from prison and goes to Mexico, 118; witnesses sit-down strikes in Michigan, 56; writes for Hollywood under own name, 139.
WORKS-DRAMA:
Black Pit, 23, 29-32, 33
"Merry Go Round," 15–21, 22, 31, 33, 69, 140
"Morrison Case, The," 32, 118–19
Peace on Earth, 22, 23, 24–29, 31, 33, 69
"Private Hicks," 32
"Rehearsal," 32
WORKS-FILM:
Cloak and Dagger, 72
Destination Tokyo, 72
House I Live In, The, 72
Naked City, The, 72
Pride of the Marines, The, 72
This Gun for Hire, 72
Two Mules for Sister Sara, 139
WORKS-PROSE:
"Afternoon in a Jungle," 69, 71
Afternoon in the Jungle, 139
"Bodies by Fisher," 56
"Circus Come to Town," 116
"Cop, The," 139
Cross and the Arrow, The, 57, 74–85, 127, 140
"Drop-Forge Man, The," 40, 41
"Game, The," 40

"Good-by," 40–41
"Happiest Man on Earth, The," 42–44, 140
"Hotel Raleigh, the Bowery," 33, 107
"Husband and Wife," 132
"Incident on a Street Corner," 41–42, 71
Journey of Simon McKeever, The, 104–16
"Letter from the Country, A," 41, 42
Long Day in a Short Life, A, 132, 138, 140
"Man on a Road," 33, 36–37, 70, 131, 140
"Pan," 132
"Prisoner's Dog, The," 139
"Season of Celebration," 33, 34–36, 70, 71, 120
"Spoils of War, The," 139
"Sunday Morning on Twentieth Street," 69, 70, 71
Tale of One January, A, 132–38, 140
"To All People of Good Will," 47–48
Underground Stream, The, 53–69, 140
"Way Things Are, The," 38–40
Way Things Are, The, 33, 34, 36, 38, 40, 43, 69, 139
"What Shall We Ask of Writers?" 85–95
"Whiskey Men, The," 118
"With Laughter," 132
WORKS-RADIO PLAY:
"Red Head Baker,"32

MacLeish, Archibald, 91
Mann, Thomas, 100–101
Man's Fate (Malraux), 60
Marching Song (Lawson), 23
Marching! Marching! (Weatherwax), 89
McCarthy, Mary, 52
McDowell, John, 101
Menjou, Adolphe, 96
Mother (Brecht-Peters), 23
Mundt, Karl, 130

New Criticism, The, 72
New Masses, The, 50, 51
North, John, 31, 53, 91

Oak, Liston, 29
O'Brien, Edward J., 36
Ornitz, Samuel, 97, 101

Paradise Lost (Odets), 51
Partisan Review, 49–51
Phillips, William, 52
Pilgrim's Progress (Bunyan), 107
Precedent (Golden), 17
Prescott, Orville, 84

Rabkin, Gerald, 29
Rahv, Philip, 52
Rand, Ayn, 97
Rankin, John, 95–96, 102
Reid, Ogden, 128
Rideout, Walter, 93
Rogers, Lela, 96
Rothstein, Arthur, 17

Sailors of Cattaro (Wolf), 23, 28
Schneider, Isidor, 53, 85–88, 90–91
Schumach, Murray, 128–29
Scott, Adrian, 97, 101
Shannon, David, 93
Shenton, James, 46
Sillen, Samuel, 84, 85, 92
Sinatra, Frank, 130, 131, 132
Sklar, George, 15, 16, 17, 21, 22, 73
Smith, Gerald L.K., 99
Smith, Lillian, 90
Social Justice, 46, 47, 48
Steinbeck, John, 42, 47, 53
Stevedore (Peters and Sklar), 23, 28

Stevenson, Philip, 34
Strauss, Harold, 60

Taylor, Robert, 96
Theatre Union, The, 22–24, 29
Thomas, J. Parnell, 96, 98, 102
Thompson, Ralph, 69
Truman, Harry S. 103
Trumbo, Dalton, 53, 73, 97, 98, 101, 103, 129

Understanding Poetry (Brooks and Warren), 73

Vansittart, Baron Robert Gilbert, 7475, 82

Waiting for Godot (Beckett), 35
Waiting for Nothing (Kromer), 34, 35, 49
Watch on the Rhine (Hellman), 89
We Hold These Truths, 46
Walker, Charles, 22, 23
Walker, James, 17, 18
Walter, Francis E. 128
Wechsler, James, 47
Whicher, George F., 85
Whitman, Walt, 74
Wilder, Thornton, 72
Wilson, Edmund, 51
Wright, Richard, 42, 47, 53, 90

Young, Stark, 16